*W*ishing

---

glorious bouquets

of flowers to nurture

the spirit of love.

A Fireside Book

NEW YORK LONDON TORONTO SYDNEY SINGAPORE

Flowers Are for Love

A BOUQUET

OF INSPIRATIONAL

STORIES

Kathy Lamancusa

FIRESIDE

ROCKEFELLER CENTER

1230 AVENUE OF THE AMERICAS

NEW YORK, NY 10020

Designed by Barbara M. Bachman

MANUFACTURED IN THE UNITED STATES OF AMERICA

1 3 5 7 9 10 8 6 4 2

LIBRARY OF CONGRESS CATALOGING-IN-PUBLICATION DATA

LAMANCUSA, KATHY.

FLOWERS ARE FOR LOVE : A BOUQUET OF INSPIRATIONAL STORIES /

KATHY LAMANCUSA.

P.   CM.

1. LOVE—MISCELLANEA. 2. FLOWERS—MISCELLANEA. I. TITLE.

HQ801 .L275 2001

306.7—DC21

00-050352

ISBN 0-7432-0608-8

Acknowledgments

...

THE FIRST EXPRESSION OF GRATITUDE MUST GO TO the contributors who have shared their stories so that others can experience that twittering of the heart that is the true essence of love. Each found that the special moments of their romantic lives were greatly impacted by the scent and beauty of flowers, and I appreciate their desire to share their moments with our readers.

Cherise Grant, my editor at Simon & Schuster, has been an angel throughout the process of compiling this book. I have appreciated her dedication, professionalism, and most important, her spirit. Her guidance and direction have impacted the messages shared and will certainly make a profound impact with our readers. Cherise, you are one class act—a lady of style, grace, and spirit.

I am so grateful to Peter Miller, of the Peter Miller Film & Literary Agency, who has been an incredible asset during the process of development. He connected with my vision of the project from the very beginning and has assisted in so many ways to bring my dream to fruition. Elaine Gartner of PMA was my fairy godmother, helping in more ways than I can possibly mention, from editing the original proposal to helping secure stories from her list of clients, family, and friends.

My sister-in-law and business associate, Katherine Lamancusa, receives my deepest appreciation for her professionalism and dedication to the details of the project. Her ability to jump in at the last minute with a laser-sharp focus assisted in bringing this book in on deadline, for which I am eternally grateful.

I want to also thank Kelly Rasile for her help with the beginning stages of this book. Her strong editing abilities helped to make this a better book. I'm thrilled that Malinda Oakes has joined our office to handle contributor relations and future book projects.

My friend Terry Paulson, Ph.D., has the ability to see deeply into the human spirit, make sense of what he sees, and share that which is most beautiful with others in ways that can be understood and appreciated. His assistance with one of the stories in this book enhanced its beauty and strengthened its message of hope. I am grateful for his willingness to always be there when needed on the journey.

The largest expression of appreciation must go to God, who has allowed me to be His messenger of flowers to the world. He speaks to us through flowers, and when we listen to the message he shares, we are energized. God wants us to use His gift of flowers to make a difference in the lives of many.

I want to dedicate this book to my husband, Joe,

who allows me the time to follow the unpaved

pathways of life I can't help but notice, and helps

nurture and grow opportunities that make

a difference in people's lives.

From a moment of locked eyes during a spinning

dance at a college in Cleveland, through raising two

remarkable sons, and into a life of empty nesting,

we have traveled the road together—"during good

times and bad, in sickness and health,

till death do us part"—with a mutual commitment

to God and each other. Your love is important

to me . . . as are you. . . . I love you!

Contents

...

Introduction

*Bread feeds the body indeed,
but flowers feed also the soul.*

—THE KORAN

Flowers Are for Love is the second book in our inspirational story series. I am so honored that our first book, *Flowers Are Forever,* has been so widely received. As I traveled the country sharing the stories that it contains, I was continually reminded of the depth and breadth of the emotions that flowers evoke in different people. Words from the introduction of the first book guided me as I presented messages of the beauty of flowers to thousands of people. Let me share them with you:

> *Flowers help us celebrate; they inspire our passions, send messages of love and romance, and brighten our days during times of sorrow, illness, and depression. A fresh bouquet is a long-distance hug, a spirit lifter, and a stress reliever, providing us with a moment of calm in our hectic lives. Many of life's passages— from birth to death and all the joyous and bittersweet*

moments in between—are marked by the giving and receiving of flowers. The sight or scent of a particular bloom often causes a flood of emotion-packed memories of a certain time, place, or person. The flowers themselves may not actually last forever, but the memories they evoke most certainly do.

As I share these words with my audiences, I continue to be surprised by the impact they have. In Kansas City, a woman in tears told me her story. It seems that every week for the last few years of her mother's life, she bought her mother flowers. Her mother always told her not to waste her money on the flowers, since they would just die soon enough. The young woman told her mother that she wanted her to enjoy the flowers while she was living. She said that when her mother died she would just pick a bucket of dandelions and throw them over the coffin. Since her mother wouldn't be able to enjoy the flowers, they wouldn't need to be beautiful. She told me that her mother passed away this year and she kept her promise up to the end. A bucket of dandelions was picked and she threw them over the coffin—knowing that her mother had enjoyed the true beauty of flowers while she lived.

I must admit that I get that comment a lot—"But flowers die." Yes, my friends, flowers do wilt and fade away. However, like anything in our hectic, material world, if something lasts for a long time, we tend to not appreciate it anymore. That is perhaps the true, fleeting beauty of flowers. They don't last forever, which forces us to appreciate them now—

while they are living and adding spirit and energy to our daily lives.

Over fifty contributors have joined me in *Flowers Are for Love,* to again share the profound message of flowers. These contributors are prominent floral designers, influential floral industry members, motivational speakers, inspirational leaders, creative consultants, and everyday flower and garden lovers. They are a true inspiration to me and have taught me so much about the deep inner connection of flowers to our souls. Walk along the path again with them, and me, as we all explore together the impact flowers have on our lives, this time in the area of romance.

As with *Flowers Are Forever,* I've included practical floral care and handling secrets, along with gardening tips and techniques. All of this is carefully designed to assist you in seeing the beauty in the world more clearly through the inspiration of flowers while helping you more thoroughly enjoy gardening and floral display. The inspirational material will help you understand the deep impact flowers have on our hearts and souls.

I'm looking forward to sharing the incredible stories from this second volume, as well as preparing a third book for which we are collecting stories. Look in the back of this book for contact information. I'm sure that you have a floral story to share.

chapter one

Romantic Celebrations

BLOSSOMS ARE SCATTERED BY THE WIND

AND THE WIND CARES NOTHING,

BUT THE BLOSSOMS OF THE

HEART NO WIND CAN TOUCH.

—*Yoshida Kenko*

THE TEN-COW WIFE
Rochelle Beach

. . .

I FIRST HEARD THIS TALE OF JOHNNY LINGO several years ago, when I was the director of the teacher improvement classes at the Church of Jesus Christ of Latter-day Saints.

A long time ago, in a small village, the custom of the day was for a father to sell his daughters in marriage. The normal price for a wife was two or three cows. One father, believing that his daughter was less than outstanding, hoped to get at least one cow for her. The girl hung her head in the village, believing herself to be worthless, until the day Johnny Lingo appeared at her family's door. He told the girl's father that he wanted the girl to be his wife, and he offered eight cows for her. Everyone in the village was shocked, including the girl. But two years later, when Johnny and his wife came back to the village, the villagers were even more surprised by the dramatic changes in the girl. She was beautiful and held her head high with pride. She became the most revered woman in the village.

Over the years, this story has become important to me and my husband. I suffered from low self-esteem, having come from a home where I received very little support or praise. My husband, John, on the other hand, grew up in a home where support was given freely. In many ways, he has become my Johnny Lingo and has allowed me to grow and

flourish in the warmth of his love. We wanted more than anything to spread our love by building a family of our own. We
were already the proud parents of a little girl and we desperately wanted another child. But after two pregnancies ended
in miscarriages, I sank into a deep and consuming depression.
Following the second miscarriage, I became physically ill on
top of the emotional strain. I was truly a mess.

One afternoon when I was feeling extremely down and
questioning my self-worth, the doorbell rang. I dragged myself
to the door and cheerlessly opened it. Standing there with the
biggest and most colorful bouquet of flowers I'd ever seen was
a deliveryman from the local florist shop. I stood there for a
moment, my mouth hanging open wordlessly, when he reluctantly said, "I really hope you won't be too upset by this." As
he spoke, I noticed that the flowers had been arranged around
a stuffed cow. I opened the card and read: "To my ten-cow
wife." Ten cows! John wanted me to know that I was worth
more to him than even Johnny Lingo's wife. Tears of happiness
streamed down my cheeks. Those flowers and their message
couldn't have come at a better time!

I later called the flower shop to explain the meaning of
the card to the florist, who must have been worrying that it
was something offensive. As the florist listened to the story
she began to cry, and she told the other people in the shop
about Johnny Lingo. Pretty soon we were all in tears!

My husband taught me, as well as the folks at the flower
shop, a lot that day. By telling me how much I mean to him,
by continually supporting me and helping me move into a
more positive frame of mind, he helped me begin to think bet-

ter of myself again. John truly is my Johnny Lingo. I no longer hang my head or question my self-worth; through his eyes, I was able to lift myself up and become the person I am.

ORCHIDS APPEAR TO REQUIRE A LOT OF MAIN-tenance, but they're really no more difficult to care for than other potted plants. Because they are native to tropical and subtropical regions, tropicslike conditions must be provided for them to grow and bloom indoors. Cattleya, Dendrobium, Oncidium, and Phalaenopsis are probably the easiest to grow.

Orchids are epiphytes—plants that live non-parasitically on other plants, such as trees and bushes. Nutrients and water from rain, air, decaying plant material, and dust, not elements from soil, are absorbed through their long, fleshy roots.

Potted orchids require bark chips, sphagnum moss, compost, clay or terra-cotta fragments, charcoal chips, small pieces of polystyrene, or a combination of any of these to grow in. The chosen potting medium must allow for good aeration of the plants' roots.

Orchids prefer plenty of bright indirect light

but should be protected from direct sun. Western and southern exposures are favored. Phalaenopsis orchids prefer a shaded eastern exposure.

Daytime temperatures between 70 and 78 degrees, with nighttime temperatures around 65 degrees, are best.

Humidifiers, large bowls of water, or water-filled pebble trays placed near or under orchid plants can be used to provide additional humidity to the environment, especially during the winter months.

Orchids should not be watered every day. They should be watered well and then allowed to dry out. A good rule of thumb is to water once a week in the winter and twice a week in the summer.

If fertilizers are used, they must be diluted. A better option is to use a fertilizer that is specially prepared for orchids (20:5:10). It is best to fertilize once or twice a week during a plant's growth and blooming period.

PEONIES (*PAEONIA*) ARE AMONG THE LONGEST-LIVED of all perennials. They are remarkably hardy in a variety of climates. They like full sun but do well in moderate shade. They stay in bloom for only a week or two in the spring.

Cut stems long when buds are still tight. Each day after, snip off a little at the bottom of the stem to allow fresh water to nourish the bloom. Rinse off the ants that seem to colonize by each bush. The ants feed on the sugary nectar exuded by the buds just before they open. The ants provide protection for the bloom, keeping away bud-eating pests.

Peonies should be planted in fertile soil in the fall before the first hard frost. Place the bare-root tubers in a two-feet-deep and two-feet-across hole in a well-drained, sunny spot away from tree roots.

The tuber should be no more than two inches below the surface (one inch in warm-weather areas) with the tuber's "eyes" facing upward.

Peonies don't need to be divided frequently, just every seven to ten years.

A peony ring can be used to stake full-blossomed flowers. If such a ring is put in place early in the season the emerging foliage will hide the ring.

I am the vine, ye are the branches;
he that abideth in Me, and I in him,
the same bringeth forth much fruit;
for without Me ye can do nothing.

—JOHN 15:5

FRIVOLOUS NECESSITIES
Karen Wingard

• • •

TWENTY-NINE YEARS AGO I DELIVERED OUR first child—a baby boy. Gosh, was his daddy proud! You could see the excitement all over his face. During my five-day hospital stay I realized that all the other new mothers were receiving flowers from their husbands. Not me. I'd gotten flowers from friends and relatives, but nothing from the father of my son.

I tried to understand the reason. My husband is a physically strong man (a former Marine and a Vietnam veteran) with integrity and high morals. He was raised by third-generation Swiss who had been in this country only a short time; they were fine, honest, churchgoing folks, but very frugal. Purchasing flowers that would soon die, eating at a restaurant when there was food at home to prepare, having two or three pairs of shoes when one pair would suffice—he saw these things as unnecessary, and therefore unacceptable. And though I understood that he was just put together that way, there were times when I wanted him to go out on a limb and do something frivolous. But frivolity was not something my husband would come upon alone; it would take some kind of miracle.

My husband and I were taught to attend church regularly, and we continued that practice with our young son. We were good people doing good things and living good lives, but missing the point of "going to church." In the same way that God opens a flower bud ever so slowly and lovingly, so did He open up our hearts, and hearts that are open to Jesus miraculously begin to soften. That's what happened to my husband. As time went on, with his now-softened heart, he began to understand that although frivolous necessities are not "necessary" in life-sustaining terms, they are "necessary" in terms of the heart and soul.

Now my sunroom and dining room are filled with plants that remind us of milestones in our marriage: a twenty-fifth wedding anniversary, a fiftieth birthday, and a thirtieth wedding anniversary. It was a thrill to receive these plants, but it was the sweet way in which they were presented that stays with me. For each turning point in our lives together, I was taken away for the weekend, destination unknown. At the end of our mystery tour, there would be a plant and flowers waiting for me. On our thirtieth anniversary, for example, a plant, fresh flowers, and a bottle of wine were waiting for me in a Jacuzzi suite in New York.

The miracle of softened hearts that we experienced was

the work of God. The love we have between us has always been enough, but the things that were once considered "unnecessary" have become fun, a joy to give and an even greater joy to receive.

My husband of thirty-one years is a man after God's own heart. I am very proud of him.

HAND-TIED ROSE BOUQUETS LOOK VERY ELE-gant and are fairly easy to assemble. To retain its fresh look, the bouquet should be created the day it will be used.

Use between twelve and twenty slightly opened roses. Remove all the foliage and thorns from each stem. To add support to the stem, cut a 20-gauge floral wire one-half inch longer than the rose stem. Place the wire along the stem and push about one-half inch of the wire into the base of the rose head. Starting near the base of the flower head, wrap the wire and stem together with floral tape. Repeat this process with all the flowers.

Place all of the roses together into a group to form the full bouquet. Intersperse foliage such as baker fern and baby's breath between the roses.

About three to four inches below the bottommost flower heads, tape the stems together for a few inches, forming a handle. Cover the taped rose stems by wrapping with 1-inch-wide ribbon and finish with a two-loop bow.

*You willingly acknowledge some possibility
of angels' existence because they have the
tact to stay invisible. Or you feign to believe
in them and it is easy to deny them,
whereas a poppy, an oak or a service tree
(sorb) has the effrontery to affirm, with
insupportable evidence, the presence
of an impossible dream.*

—ANDRÉ DHÔTEL

GROWING ROOTS
Diane Gunn Hurd

. . .

I FOUND MYSELF SITTING IN AN OFFICE WITH
my boss and the director of Personnel while the two of them
squirmed, trying to explain why my position of fifteen years
was being eliminated. The strange thing is that instead of feeling shocked or upset, I felt a sense of indescribable joy and
relief pass through me. I knew that my life carried so much
more promise and purpose than I'd been able to cultivate
while tied into this huge big-pocket/small-heart corporation.

While playing my role in corporate America, I didn't
make any serious commitments or start a family of my own.
I had been more concerned with my job and where it would
take me, always hoping and waiting for the next relocation or

promotion. Over the past years, I'd lived in New York; Los Angeles; Washington, D.C.; and London. My roots didn't grow very deep, and I was tired of transplanting myself. But now my life was about to change. And I was ready.

Before plunging back into the workforce, I decided to take a sabbatical. I went to a yoga ashram and retreat site in upstate New York, where I did volunteer work. From there, I planned on going to India for an extended stay to study yoga and Eastern scriptures, to visit sacred temples, and to walk the streets and villages where saints and sages of ancient times had made their pilgrimages. My severance pay would cover a year in upstate New York, as well as a year in India.

One afternoon, six months later, while I was reading a book as I waited for a bus at the shuttle stop in the ashram, a tall and handsome strawberry-blond man politely asked me if the bus he was looking for stopped there. His manners were the first thing that impressed me, and his gentle demeanor seemed familiar and safe. During our brief conversation, I learned that he had come for a week.

Over the course of his one-week stay, we would talk many more times. His name was John, and he was a farmer from Wisconsin who grew flowers and had his own dried flower wholesale business. It sounded so peaceful and beautiful, isolated from the hustle and bustle of the city life I was used to, surrounded by nature. And the better I got to know John, the more I longed to visit his farm someday.

We exchanged addresses and wrote to each other twice before his next one-week visit in July. And when he returned, we spent the week having meals together and meeting for chats and chai. The feelings between us began to stir. This put me in a difficult spot. I was scheduled to leave for India in just three months—it was a trip I had been planning for a long, long time. I couldn't afford to have feelings for someone right then, especially someone I hardly knew. When the week was over, John traveled back to Wisconsin and I daydreamed about writing exciting, adventure-filled letters to him from India. Then I was struck with fear. *Suppose John meets someone else while I am in India,* I thought. But I set the fear aside and tried to banish all thoughts about John, the farm, the flowers, and Wisconsin. I needed to concentrate on India.

I couldn't. I kept remembering John's gentle voice and imagining him in fields of bountiful, fragrant flowers. I became angry. "Why," I asked myself, "did I have to meet someone so special just when I am about to leave for India for a year?" I tried to bury myself with other concerns. Instead I became very ill and was forced to stay in bed for almost a week. My body decided to shut down until my mind would deal with the new emotions that were flooding it. While feverishly struggling to put John out of my mind, I suddenly realized that there was a pattern to all of my relationships. Whenever I met someone I really cared for, I moved away. Or perhaps it was because I was moving away that I began to really care about someone. I decided that it was time to change this pattern.

I called John. He was pleasantly surprised to hear from me, and he didn't waste any time before telling me that he missed me immensely and had been thinking about me since he left. He explained that he had wanted to invite me to Wisconsin but didn't because I was going to India. I told him that I would come if he invited me. He did, and we began to plan our rendezvous.

We scheduled a week together in September and began the journey of getting to know one another. I arrived full of excitement and anticipation, and as we entered the driveway into the farm, driving past acres of corn and rows of hydrangeas, I could see his beautiful old stone house that looked full of history and character.

The first day on the farm, John had to tend to chores, so I remained in the old house and peered out of the porch windows into a world I did not recognize. I felt lost and disoriented. But when John returned and made us some herbal tea, I slowly began to loosen up and feel more comfortable. We spent hours talking and laughing and learning about one another. On the second day, I thought, *I could live here.* On the third day, I caught myself noticing that there was room for me and for all of my furniture in John's house. Before the end of a week, we realized that we were in love and that there was an indescribable bond—a knowing that we should be together. We decided that we didn't want to live apart—especially on separate continents!

A year and a half has passed since I moved to Wisconsin. John is my best friend, a man I admire and respect, a man with courage, integrity, depth, and character. I run the dried flower wholesale business and help on the farm as often as I can. We were married in the West Indies on the island of St. Kitts on March 11, 2000. It was a small, personal, and beautiful wedding with only sixteen of our closest friends and family. It was the happiest day of my life, one I will always treasure.

In the first month and a half of our marriage we planted, cultivated, and hoed over three thousand young flower bushes, and pruned over two thousand hydrangea bushes. We then began to harvest two acres of peonies. We have worked on advertisements, a web site, an upcoming trade show, and a new price list, as well as making decisions about which new flowers and products we will grow and buy next year. With this new life, I have been able to enjoy things I had never experienced during my years of corporate employment. At no other job have I been able to have my favorite cats lounging on my desk in the office, and I certainly never found wildlife—gophers, ferrets, and groundhogs—in the supply room while looking for staples. I've never had a job that paid me to be in the sunshine all day, with the wind in my face and birds and squirrels at my feet. My previous jobs never exposed me to the splendor of nature: a mother killdeer looking after her unhatched babies; the beauty of geese and cranes; deer pausing, eating, and fleeing. I have never before shared space with a workforce of bees and fluttering butterflies. Every day is filled with new and beautiful things, and I am fortunate enough to watch and participate in the dance of nature.

I am very grateful for that day in March '98, when the love of my life entered my life with the tenderness of a spring day and with the impact of a thunderbolt, opening my heart and my eyes to a world I had only known secondhand. Flowers now occupy my thoughts, my focus, my time, and my imagination. I feel that they are part of my destiny. When I wander through acres of fragrant, colorful blossoms, I can't help but feel blessed for being alive and in love. And for finally knowing that my roots are firmly planted—for good.

THE DAMASK, OR BULGARIAN, ROSE, WITH ITS rich, heady aroma, is a popular choice for fine fragrances. This is remarkable when you consider that it takes four thousand pounds of damask roses to extract just one pound of oil.

AROMATHERAPY, USING ESSENTIAL OILS TO HEAL the body and mind, has been practiced since ancient Egyptian times. The key to aromatherapy is the essential oil, which is the aromatic component of a plant.

The use of scented candles, health, and beauty products would be better described as aromacology, which is the use of a smell to trigger a reaction caused by memory. The effects of scent are dependent on the user's memories.

Aromatherapy basic essential oils are believed to provide the following benefits to mind and body:

BASIL —*for mental and physical fatigue; aids in mental alertness and concentration*

BERGAMOT —*a citrus/floral note, fruity and warm; combats fatigue, tension, and anxiety*

CHAMOMILE —*has sedative and stress-relieving qualities*

CLARY SAGE —*balances menstrual and menopausal difficulties*

CYPRESS —*an evergreen oil and astringent; may be useful for circulatory and respiratory problems*

EUCALYPTUS —*aids respiratory ailments and stimulates circulation; increases blood flow and concentration*

GERANIUM —*has a hormonal balancing effect*

GINGER —*strong, spicy-sweet scent; for aching muscles*

JUNIPER —*cleans the atmosphere of a room*

LAVENDER —*has more uses than any other oil; relieves insect bite irritation, calms, relieves stress, balances emotions, and eases pain*

LEMON —*germicide and astringent*

PEPPERMINT —*revitalizes and stimulates the body and mind; has a stimulating effect on circulation and the digestive system*

PINE —*has infection-fighting properties*

SANDALWOOD —*meditation aid and aphrodisiac*

YLANG-YLANG —*antidepressant; relaxes the body, mind, and spirit*

Consider the lilies how they grow: they toil not,
they spin not; and yet I say unto you,
that Solomon in all his glory was not arrayed
like one of these.

—Luke 12:27

DRIED AND TRUE
Christina Keating

. . .

I MET PHIL DURING MY FIRST SEMESTER OF college. We quickly became very close friends, and eventually we began dating. We had plenty of ups and downs over the next five years, fighting and then making up, separating and then getting back together. And during those years, Phil frequently sent me flowers, sometimes for no other reason than that he was thinking of me. For reasons I can't begin to fathom, I dried and saved every bouquet he sent me. I had never done anything like that before; I'd always simply admired the flowers while they were alive and thrown them away when they were wilted and dead. And even though Phil would jokingly poke fun at me for keeping them, it was just something I did.

Almost six years to the day after we met, Phil proposed. I happily accepted and eagerly began planning "the most important day of my life." One day, while I was cleaning out my room in preparation for moving out of my parents' house, I came across all of the roses that I had been saving. I sat on my floor, pulling the petals off of the stems, one by one, and placing them in a basket. It was then that I realized what I had been saving these flowers for. The flowers that had been given for "Thinking of you," "I'm sorry," "I love you," and "Just because you're you" were blended together with fresh rose petals from the flowers he sent me the morning of our wedding, the day toward which all of those feelings had led us. And as the flower girls walked down the aisle, they tossed that beautiful bouquet of old and new and always along my path, leading me to that wonderful, thoughtful man I'd always meant to marry.

FLOWERS CAN BE DRIED BY SIMPLY GATHERING THE fresh flowers into a grouping before their heads begin to droop, wrapping their stems with a rubber band, and hanging the bunch upside down in a dark, dry, cool location, allowing the flowers to dry out naturally. Another method involves removing the heads from the flowers and placing them in a shallow box with space around each flower for airflow. Place the box in a dry, cool location.

*Flowers leave some of their
fragrance in the hand
that bestows them.*

—CHINESE PROVERB

SENSUAL FLOWERS
Kathy G. Wise

. . .

ONE OF MY FONDEST CHILDHOOD MEMORIES is that of my grandfather giving my mother beautiful bouquets of fresh snapdragons, gladiolas, bachelor buttons, and peonies. I loved to watch the two of them exchange smiles; he enjoyed giving her the flowers as much as she enjoyed receiving them. Seeing this as a child made me realize that something as simple as the gift of flowers can brighten even the worst of days. My husband, John, has realized it, too. He knows that I love flowers as much as my mother did, and that giving or receiving them can always make me smile. One day I decided to see if flowers would bring a smile to his face as well.

The day had been a rough one, my husband explained when I called to touch base. An attorney, he was working on a very difficult case, and nothing was going right for him. I could hear the distress in his voice, yet there was nothing I could do to help him. "I hope things get better," I said before hanging up, and told him that I had confidence in his ability to get it all worked out. Still bothered by our conversation, though, I found it impossible to concentrate on my own work. I couldn't stop thinking about him, and I wished there was something I could do to make him feel better. That's when it hit me: Why not send my husband flowers? I called my florist and told her what I wanted to do. I asked her if sending flowers to a man was all right, wondering if it was a "masculine" thing to do. She assured me that many women send men flowers and that it is a perfectly acceptable gesture. So we discussed types of flowers and decided on birds of paradise because they have a nice, strong, masculine appearance. I picked out the perfect colors, added a provocative note, and asked to have them delivered that afternoon. I was very excited. I could hardly wait until he received the flowers and called to respond to my sexy note.

I waited and waited. No call. At four o'clock, I decided to call him.

"Hi, honey, is your day getting better?" I asked.

"Yes, a little better. I think I've got it all worked out, but it put me behind," he explained.

"Anything new or exciting happen this afternoon?" I asked.

"No, not really," he said. This was not the answer I was hoping for, and I suddenly wondered if the florist had misunderstood my order. I had said that afternoon, hadn't I? Finally, I just asked him if he'd received anything out of the ordinary.

"Did you send me flowers?" he asked, surprised.

When I told him that I had, he thanked me and told me

he loved them. He then reluctantly admitted that since he had sometimes received unwanted advances from women he worked with professionally, he hadn't known for certain if the flowers were from me—I'd forgotten to sign the card, he informed me, and he thought maybe he had a secret admirer he would rather not know about.

"You wish," I said, and we both laughed.

I learned two very important things that day. First, men love getting flowers as much as women do. Second, and most pertinent, if you're going to send flowers with sensual notes, you'd better sign the card.

LADY MARY WORTLEY MONTAGU, WIFE OF THE British ambassador in Constantinople, is credited with creating the language of flowers in western Europe. On March 16, 1718, she sent a letter to a friend in Britain that said, "I have got for you as you desire, a Turkish love letter, which I have put in a box, and ordered the Captain of the Smyrniote to deliver it to you with this letter." Lady Montagu further explained the meanings of the roses, jonquils, cloves, straw, and other botanicals she included in the form of a tussie-mussie.

Lady Montagu wrote, "There is no flower

without a verse belonging to it; and it is possible to quarrel, reproach, or send letters of passion, friendship, or civility, or even of news without even inking your fingers."

Flowers presented in this form reached a peak of popularity during Victorian times. By the early 1800s members of the French court had what they called *le langage des fleurs*, and the Germans were referring to *Blumen-Sprache*.

MANY CUT ROSES LACK SCENT, BUT THERE ARE a few varieties with good fragrance: Fragrant Cloud and Tropicana, two orange rose varieties; and Mr. Lincoln and L. B. Braithwaite, both red roses.

Flowers get their scent from substances known as volatile compounds—essential oils found primarily on the surface of petals. Scent actually is an aspect of flower evolution, a characteristic that might repel pests or attract desirable insects such as moths, which spread pollen.

A given flower might have dozens of volatile compounds that evaporate in warm conditions to form a distinctive scent. Roses, for example, have a large number; orchids can have more than one hundred such compounds. Researchers now are looking at flower genes for enzymes that form volatile compounds. This work could lead to ways of manipulating genes to produce a desired scent.

ONE LEGEND DESCRIBING TEA ROSES SAYS THAT they were so named because their aroma is reminiscent of the finest tea. Another legend says that the name came about because the roses and tea were shipped together, and therefore were named together.

I only went out for a walk and finally
concluded to stay out till sundown,
for going out, I found, was really going in.

—JOHN MUIR

A ROSE FOR DARYL
Larry Laney

. . .

IT HAD BEEN A VERY LONG AND COLD WINTER. When spring finally rolled around I took a tally of what remained of my prized rose garden. Well, I like to think of it as a prized rose garden, but in reality it was a garden of hopes and dreams; my wife, Daryl, and I had been desperately trying to nurture a beautiful garden for more than two years. Sadly, all of the rosebushes we had planted were dead except one, and even the survivor was not much to look at—quite small and very frostbitten. I'm a pretty optimistic guy, though, and I still hoped and prayed that that miserable little bush would surprise me with a bouquet of beautiful roses. To my disappointment, only one bud appeared. But as time passed that small bud transformed into a beautiful rose. I visited that single rose every day, sometimes sitting for a few minutes admiring its beauty. I knew it wouldn't be long before it began to fade and die. I hoped there would be more buds, but one good look at the bush told me it was not going to survive. This was probably the only rose it would ever produce.

On the day when the rose was at its fullest and most beautiful, it suddenly dawned on me that Mother's Day had arrived and I had forgotten to buy my lovely wife, Daryl, a present. She seldom complained about my insensitivity and bad memory, but I was pretty sure she was expecting a gift. What was I to do? I'm sure that many men have experienced this at least once or twice in their married life. Husbands know, just as I did at that moment, that forgetting Mother's Day is not a smart thing for any married man to do.

I thought about jumping into my pickup truck, hurrying to town, and buying a gift. Any gift was better than no gift at this late date. *That's what I'll do,* I thought. *I'll go to town and quickly find a gift for Daryl, before she ever knows I forgot.*

As I was hurrying to my truck I passed the rosebush. The beauty of that one single bloom stopped me once again. It sure was pretty! I started heading to the truck, but then a thought came to me. What better way to show Daryl how much I loved and admired her than to give her that single rose.

I hurried to the barn and found the rose clippers. I quickly returned to the rosebush, determined to cut that rose for my wife. It wasn't easy to cut the stem. I sat there for over half an hour looking at that rose. I thought, *This rose is beautiful, and there will probably never be another like this one.* But the real flower in my life was my wife. She brightened my life more than any flower ever could. How would she feel? I had a hidden fear that she would think I was cheap because I was giving her only a single rose. But I reasoned that Daryl knew how I felt about the failed rose garden and the single rose from a doomed bush, and I prayed that she would understand the importance of this gift. I eventually cut the rose and presented it to her in a small vase. I nervously waited for her reaction.

She looked at the rose and then at me. To my relief, a smile appeared and tears began streaming down her face. She gave me a big hug and a long, passionate kiss. She said, "You loved me enough to give me your only rose."

Daryl and I are still very happily married and still trying to grow a rose garden.

chapter two

The Gift of Flowers

BUT WHEN THOU DOEST ALMS, LET NOT THY
LEFT HAND KNOW WHAT THY RIGHT HAND
DOETH: THAT THINE ALMS MAY BE IN SECRET:
AND THY FATHER WHICH SEETH IN SECRET
HIMSELF SHALL REWARD THEE OPENLY.

—Matthew 6:3-4

LOVE, UN-AMERICAN-STYLE
Hope Mihalap

. . .

"HOW OLD IS YOUR GRANDMOTHER?" HE asked. I had no idea that this was the prelude to a marriage proposal.

"She's ninety-two."

"She needs a great-grandchild. Let's get married."

I had just cooked a chicken at my Russian professor's apartment, at his request. This was our first date after a year-long Russian course, at the end of which I wasn't sure if he even remembered my last name. But he had asked me to dinner, then asked if I could cook. I accepted his curious invitation and told him that I could indeed cook, to which he responded, "I have a chicken," and hung up.

I supposed that my parents wouldn't be thrilled with the idea that I was going to a relative stranger's apartment for dinner—especially in our small town, where someone might "find out." But it didn't take them long to shout their approval. Of course, that could have had something to do with the fact that I was single and twenty-nine years old, and everyone else's daughters were married. I had taken the Russian course at the local college hoping that a few bachelors would be taking the course, too. They weren't, but the professor was single and had an interesting Russian accent.

It was one thing to accept a dinner invitation, but it was

another thing altogether to accept a marriage proposal because I had cooked a chicken. "That's crazy!" I told him. "Why should we get married when we don't even know one another?"

He looked at me earnestly. "I give you two reasons," he began. "We both want to get married and we're both old."

"True," I said. "But this is a bad proposal. You haven't said anything romantic. You haven't said you love me."

"I don't love you," he said. " I barely know you."

And so began the weirdest courtship in marital lore, a courtship so devoid of the sweeping romance you read about, so unorthodox, that I couldn't just let it proceed without comment.

"I can't say yes," I snapped after a second date. "You won't say you love me. All grooms love their brides."

"Real love comes after marriage," he reasoned. "We don't know each other well enough to be in love."

No! I thought angrily to myself. *This is not what all the magazines, novels, and movies say. No! This isn't the way it's supposed to happen.* I believed that people should fall in love first and then get married—except in those European arranged marriages, which this was beginning to resemble more and more. Then again, people in those arranged marriages often ended up in love. How could this happen? It was un-American.

And so there were no boxes of candy, no phone calls, no flowers, no meaningful glances. But there were a few things I couldn't deny about this unique relationship: humor, originality, and a certain suspense.

We got married on a Thanksgiving Day. Exactly one week later, he brought me six roses.

"Happy Thursday anniversary!" he exclaimed joyously.

And exclaimed again the next Thursday, and the next, and the next, culminating on our first year's anniversary, when he brought me a dozen roses, still fresh in the vase when our daughter was born a week later. After the first few months of Thursday bouquets I told him how romantic that sentiment was, and asked why he hadn't done this type of thing before we were married.

"Because you might have said no," he replied, "and I would have wasted all that money."

NEGLECTED ROSES CAN BE REJUVENATED WITH careful pruning and dedicated attention. Older bushes should be vigorously pruned, stimulating rejuvenation. Never prune in freezing weather. In warm areas of the country, roses should be pruned during the coolest months. This will allow them a chance to store energy before they bloom again.

Roses need attention throughout the year to continue abundant growth. New and established roses should be pruned in early spring at the first signs of growth. Straggly, overly long shoots should be pruned mid-spring. To encourage new growth in the summer months, gardeners should dead-head faded blooms and prune any storm-damaged stems. In early fall, cut away dead, straggly, or diseased stems.

THE FLOWERS WE COMMONLY CALL ROSES ARE in the *Rosa* genus and belong to the Rosaceae family, which includes more than twenty thousand cultivars of the world's most popular cut flowers. Their beauty is timeless, and the blossoms originated more than four thousand years ago in the fertile land between the Tigris and Euphrates Rivers in the Middle East. Today, florist's roses are available in three types: sweetheart, spray, and tea.

Four states and the District of Columbia list roses as their official flower. The District of Columbia favors the American beauty rose; Georgia celebrates the Cherokee rose; Iowa honors the wild rose; and North Dakota has adopted the wild prairie rose. New York loves all types and styles of roses and simply lists "rose," instead of naming a favorite variety.

And he shall be like a tree planted
by rivers of water, that bringeth forth
his fruit in his season.

—PSALMS 1:3

TWO CORSAGES
Arnold "Nick" Carter

. . .

AS A POOR COLLEGE STUDENT AT SYRACUSE University, I was lucky if I had two nickels to rub together. As luck would have it, I was madly in love with a very attractive and very wealthy young woman, a Syracuse coed. There was a big dance coming up, and I asked her to be my date. This woman reminded me in some ways of Marie Antoinette. She had no understanding of the struggle that life can be for many people, including me, living paycheck to paycheck, so I never let on that I was one of those people. She accepted my invitation, and I somehow managed to scrimp and save enough money to buy her a rather meager corsage. I knew it wasn't much, and probably less magnificent than she was expecting, but it was all I could afford; I just hoped my efforts would be appreciated.

When the big night came, I arrived and sheepishly handed her the corsage. I could not have predicted her reaction! Expecting an opulent floral treatment and receiving my meager attempt, she slammed the flowers to the floor with a vicious swing of her arm, incensed and disgusted. She had expected more than I was able to give her. When I broke down and explained that I was just a poor college student, she was extremely angry with me for pretending to be what I wasn't: rich. In her eyes I was a fake, a phony, a student of little means acting well-to-do. I understand now that I probably shouldn't have been mingling outside of my own class, so to speak. I probably got what I deserved. Love is blind, but I suddenly wasn't. I realized how foolish I'd been, and from that day forward I never again pretended to be anything I wasn't. I became painfully aware of the significant differences between those with money and those without. She had grown up in a completely different world than I, and she therefore had an entirely different perspective on life. Needless to say, I never saw her again.

When I graduated from the U.S. Navy's Officer Candidate School in Rhode Island and had more money than I was accustomed to, I once again set my sights on love. With a few bucks in my pocket, I found the courage to ask a beautiful elementary schoolteacher to a dance. She accepted. When I arrived and handed her a corsage, she received it with happiness and appreciation. What a moment for me! As it turned out, this was a turning point in my life. I married that elementary teacher, whose name was Ginger, a year or so later, and we have lived happily ever after.

I learned a valuable lesson: Sometimes what you think is the right road is really just someone else's footpath. With or without money, you must pave your own way.

Two corsages: one inadequate, one life-lifting. Those corsages taught me one of the most important lessons I've ever learned and brought me to the love and happiness I had been looking for.

THERE ARE VARIETIES OF LILIES THAT ARE NOT members of genus *Lilium* yet are called lilies anyway. Several are favorites in romantic decorating:

GLORIOSA LILY — *Liliaceae*
FOXTAIL LILY — *Eremurus*
PERUVIAN LILY — *Alstroemeria*
LILY OF THE VALLEY — *Convallaria*
LILY OF THE NILE — *Agapanthus*
GUERNSEY LILY — *Nerine*

AMARYLLIS (*HIPPEASTRUM*) BLOOMS IN CLUSTERS OF three or more large, lilylike flowers ranging from eight to ten inches wide. It blooms on stems that can reach two feet in height. Strap-shaped leaves grow directly from the bulb.

An amaryllis will produce flowers each spring for up to seventy-five years with proper care.

The flowers will bloom for six to eight weeks. Repot every one to two years to encourage blooming.

THE AZALEA, WHICH BELONGS TO A SUBGENUS *(Azalea)* of rhododendrons, is a low, woody shrub with leathery, dark green leaves.

Keep the soil moist but not wet, watering directly to the root. Keep flowers and foliage dry to prevent fungal diseases. Do not fertilize. Azaleas love bright, indirect light and temperatures from 65 to 70 degrees Fahrenheit. Blooming life is two to four weeks. Dry soil, intense shade, or cool temperatures combined with intense light can cause leaves to drop. Pinch off any new green shoots that extend beyond the flowers.

I will be as the dew unto Israel;
he shall grow as the lily, and cast forth
his roots as Lebanon.

—HOSEA 14:5

THE MOST IMPORTANT COMPONENT
Susan E. Warkentin

...

I HAVE A WIDE VARIETY OF INTERESTS. FOR example, I hold a degree in mechanical engineering as well as a diploma in fashion design. These two seemingly unrelated interests blended for a year or so when I worked as an industrial engineer in a knitting mill in Toronto. It was during that time that I realized big city life was not for me.

I also have a passion for flowers that I must have inherited from my grandmother, who always had a beautiful perennial garden surrounded by a picturesque white picket fence. Even as an apartment dweller I was able to nourish my passion for flowers with tropical houseplants and balcony containers. I eventually freed myself from these constraints when I moved back to my hometown to take an engineering job in a steel fabrication plant and to get married.

Home is a small city at the base of pristine Georgian Bay in Ontario, Canada. My husband, Chris, and I purchased a house and embarked on a program of yard improvement. My husband does not share my passion for flowers and gardening, but he does like things to look neat and tidy, so he did the grunt work. It was exciting to finally have the space to experiment with plants on a larger scale. I went wild with gardening catalogs and divisions of plants from family and friends.

Chris's passions are cars, tires, and our family. In that order, I sometimes suspect. He can identify the make and model of tires from the tracks they leave in the snow. He torments car salesmen with pointed questions about the minute changes between model years. Chris gets as excited by a new tire pamphlet as I do when the new seed catalogs arrive in late winter. To be fair, he thinks my love of flowers and my ability to spout gardening trivia and identify plants are as bizarre as I find his ability to recite tire sizes with the cadence of poetry.

The manufacturing industry wasn't doing very well in rural Ontario in the late 1980s, and because Chris and I were both employed as mechanical engineers, it became clear that we needed to diversify. After much thought, I ended up going back to university to become a math and physics teacher. This entailed some risk, since teaching positions were somewhat limited, tuition was costly, and the university was hours away from home.

A few of my houseplants went with me to ease my homesickness. Chris and I were together only on weekends, when one or the other of us commuted. Many of the students in my class were older than the average postgraduate, and also married, so there was a pleasant camaraderie among us, despite the change of lifestyle. We all worked studiously, still worrying about the prospects of finding a job but hoping for the best.

I was lucky. A month following graduation I was offered a position teaching math to juniors and seniors at a high school in the next county. It would mean a total of eighty minutes of driving a day, but, we reasoned, people in the city frequently have a long drive to work, so a pleasant drive in the country wouldn't really be a hardship.

The first day of school was hectic and nerve-racking. I despaired of ever learning the names of the students in my six classes, let alone the seventy staff members. By the end of the day I felt as if I had done six one-woman shows in a row with really brutal crowds. I arrived home that evening relieved to have survived and completely exhausted. I had just collapsed on the sofa when Chris came home carrying a large package unmistakably wrapped in florist's paper. My jaw dropped and my expression must have been a toss-up between shocked and thrilled. What I unwrapped was a gorgeous basket of flowering African violets and kalanchoe nestled in ivy . . . from my husband, who always says that flowers are a waste of money! He couldn't have found a more unselfish, unexpected, or wonderful way of telling me that he had been thinking about me.

Chris must have realized how much his kind and thoughtful gesture meant to me, because gifts of flowers have grown more frequent as the years have passed. My car always has good rubber on it ("Tires are the most important component of the suspension") and my house is always filled with fabulous floral arrangements, but I suspect the gifts of tires are for Chris. And the flowers? Those are for me!

Bulbs include five different categories of plants: true bulbs, corms, tubers, rhizomes, and tuberous roots. They all share one characteristic—all are self-contained miniature bundles of energy that store their own food underground, then burst into bloom each year as soon as the temperature and moisture conditions are just right.

After flowering, the foliage dies back and nutrients are manufactured and sent to the bulb for storage for the next growing season.

Ninety percent of the bulbs we grow for flowers belong to just six genera: *Lilium, Iris, Tulipa, Hyacinthus, Narcissus,* and *Gladiolus.* Within these six are hundreds of species and thousands of varieties.

Adonis, anemone, and pulsatilla are botani-cally and horticulturally unique plants, but are all related members of the botanical family Ranunculaceae, or the buttercup family.

The genus name *Adonis* reminds us of the Greek youth with the same name, who has come to symbolize young male beauty. According to Greek mythology, Aphrodite, the goddess of love and beauty, was in love with Adonis. Ares was in love with Aphrodite and therefore jealously plotted the accidental death of Adonis.

Ares disguised himself as a wild boar and killed Adonis. A grief-stricken Aphrodite transformed Adonis's body into a flower. The blooming of the flower and its fading away are a metaphor for the premature death of Adonis.

In some versions of the story, an anemone sprang from the tears of Aphrodite as she wept over the body of Adonis. In other versions the flower sprang from the blood of Adonis.

*One touch of nature makes the
whole world kin.*

—WILLIAM SHAKESPEARE

MESSAGE ACROSS THE MILES
Poul Einshøj

...

DURING THE LATE SIXTIES I HAD A JOB
assignment that included doing research in England for six
weeks. Having to leave my home in Denmark and my fiancée
would be difficult, but just before I left things became even
more difficult. On my last day at home, my fiancée, Karen,
and I had a terrible disagreement. There was no happy departure—not a pleasant outlook for six weeks abroad without a
chance to make amends.

The first night in my rather humble west-end London flat,
trying to make sense of both the money of those days
(pounds, shillings, and pence) and a funny foreign language I
couldn't even begin to imitate, I certainly didn't feel optimistic
or encouraged about the following weeks. Plus, I hadn't heard
from my fiancée, which sent my aching mind spiraling downward until I hit the pillow and went to sleep.

Upon returning to the flat the next evening, after the first
troublesome day at work, I was met by the curious eyes of my
landlady. Having already experienced enough hardship for
one day, I decided not to return her curious stare, and went
up to my room for a bit of much-needed sleep instead. But

when I opened the door to my very basic room, I suddenly realized why the woman had been looking at me so strangely. There, illuminating the place with its very presence, was a blue bucket filled with perfect long-stemmed red roses. Stunned, it took me a moment to open the attached card that said, in Danish, "I miss you" (*Jeg Savner Dig*). Interestingly enough, things no longer seemed as bleak as they had just minutes before. Things were suddenly on the upswing, and good old England shed its clouds and became sunny for the next six weeks.

But however spectacular England had become, it was great to get back to Denmark, and back to the love of my life.

WATER IS ESSENTIAL FOR A PLANT TO SURVIVE. A cut flower must be able to drink water freely to ensure a long life. Plants have vascular systems composed of conducting cells called xylem and phloem. A flower's vascular cells help support the stem, but they also operate like a bundle of drinking straws, drawing water up the stem to the leaves and then up to the flower. It is essential to keep these cells open for water to flow freely.

A flower is composed mostly of water, and the vascular network is protected from the atmosphere by thin layers of tough cells on the stem, leaves, and petals. In dry climates, the atmosphere robs a flower of its moisture. The more humid the environment, the longer the flower will live.

Aside from tropical flowers that thrive on heat, most flowers will last longer in cool temperatures, which stabilize them. Warmth will hasten the development of flowers. Excessive cold is never good for flowers. Since the vascular system is filled with water, which expands when it freezes, the cells will burst and destroy the flower.

Always keep flowers away from excessive heat. Although we understand that we shouldn't put a flower arrangement in front of a heating vent, we sometimes forget the heat emitted from electrical equipment such as televisions and VCRs. If you want a longer life for the flowers, do not put vases on these pieces of equipment.

SINCE BATHING AND CLEANSING WERE SCARCE, Elizabethans were talented at keeping their homes sweet smelling regardless. Herbs and flowers were strewn over floors, hung from rafters, and made into potpourris.

"Just living is not enough," said the butterfly.
"One must have sunshine, freedom, and a little flower."

—HANS CHRISTIAN ANDERSEN

FIRST FLOWER
Kathy Peterson

· · ·

EVERYONE HAS A FAVORITE FLOWER. MINE IS the orchid. Not because I find it more beautiful or more fragrant than other flowers, but because it holds for me a special memory.

I had not received any flowers from a man until I was almost twenty-one years old. I'd never been invited to a prom or a dance of any kind, so I had little experience with corsages. My first flower meant a great deal because it was given to me by a well-known composer, a very dear friend who recognized my potential and helped me in many ways. His gift to me was a beautiful orchid. Sadly, shortly thereafter, my special friend died.

Seven years later I got married, and I shared the story of my first flower with my husband. I explained how that beautiful flower had affected me and how I'd preserved it in my memory. The story had a powerful effect on my husband. Later that day, I received an orchid from him with a note that said, "This being your second orchid, I hope it will mean as much as your first. Love, Tom." It did.

Fresh-cut orchids are exotic in their beauty, but surprisingly they require fairly ordinary care. Simply cut them to the desired length for the vase. You don't even have to use floral preservative.

If the stems of your orchids start to wilt, cut at least half an inch from the base of the stem. Cutting the stems underwater—in a sink or large bowl—will add to the life of the flowers. After cutting the stems, immerse the flowers, stems and all, in a warm-water bath for one to two hours.

Remove the flowers from the warm-water bath and arrange in the vase. Keep the arranged flowers away from direct sunlight and away from drafts, which cause moisture loss. Recut the stems and change the water every other day to keep the flowers fresh.

Cymbidium orchids are available in approxi- mately forty different species, from which thousands of varieties have evolved.

Cymbidium blooms range from white to yellow, yellow-green, bronze, pink, and purple.

They prefer a lot of light during the morning and late afternoon, but should be shaded from the midday sun, especially during the summer months.

You can use the leaves' color to gauge the plant's light needs. Light green leaves indicate good light, dark green leaves indicate too little light, and yellow leaves indicate too much light.

Thy two breasts are like
two young roes that are twins,
which feed among the lilies.

SONG OF SOLOMON 4:5

WHO WILL SEND
ME FLOWERS?
Jill Boudreau

. . .

MY EARLIEST MEMORY IS OF ME AS A four-year-old creating small bouquets to give to my mother. I found all the materials I needed in my grandmother's garden: forget-me-nots, miniature roses, snapdragons, comfrey, and a host of rhododendrons. And across town at my other grandmother's house, I was constantly surrounded by lilac and blueberry bushes, sweet peas, and pussy willows. I even started preserving my favorites by pressing them between the pages of big books.

It's no wonder that I became a florist. Flowers evoke a sense of comfort and innocence for me, and these very happy memories of a carefree childhood spent with my grandmas were infused into my spirit.

One day, while I was still a young college student, my mother and I were talking about my future. I told her that I would marry the man who sent me flowers. That man, I told her, would understand what flowers mean to me and would recognize my passion for flowers and floral design. And I held to that—and waited.

Then I met a United States Marine. Our first date started with dinner and a long walk along a pier near the ocean. Wanting to spend more time together, we spent the next day driving along the coast. Somehow I knew that he was special, but he still had to pass the final test. Not long into our relationship, he had to leave for six weeks of training in Georgia. Just after he left, I received a beautiful letter from him, saying that there was a place next to him for me and that he felt empty because he missed me. On Valentine's Day I arrived home after working late and found a small flower arrangement on the coffee table. The card read, "Happy Valentine's Day. Love, Dan." He'd sent me flowers.

Months turned into years of dating, and somewhere during that time I casually mentioned that I would marry the man who understood my love of flowers. Was I trying to supply him with the answer to the test? Perhaps, but I received bouquets on my birthdays, and single flowers for special occasions. And before I knew it, Dan was getting ready to leave for Desert Storm. Eight weeks after his unit sailed away I received a lovely orchid plant with a card that said, "You said you would marry the man who sent you flowers."

And so I did. Dan and I have been married for nine years and have two wonderful children. He is perfect for me; he understands my passion and knows my spirit.

ACCORDING TO A SURVEY FROM THE SOCIETY of American Florists, flowers are an easy and effective way to be romantic. Here is what women want their men to do to add romance to their lives:

41%, give or send her flowers unexpectedly
32%, cook dinner for her
10%, write her a love song or poem
8%, watch a romantic movie together
2%, feed her grapes
Fully 82% of women feel flowers are a universal
   sign of romance

THE CRAPE MYRTLE IS CALLED THE ONE-HUNDRED-day red flower in Korea.

According to legend, a three-headed sea dragon demanded that a Korean coastal village sacrifice a maiden as his bride each year. One year the town decided that the maiden would come from the house of Kim. The people dressed the chosen girl in a wedding gown and took her to the shore. As the dragon came to take her into the sea, a prince sailed in and cut off one of the dragon's heads and saved the maiden.

The father of the prince arranged for the prince and the maiden to marry, but just as the wedding day arrived the king's treasure disappeared. Angry, the king canceled the wedding. The prince promised to find the treasure within one hundred days and return to marry his bride. As he said good-bye to her, he told her he would fly a white flag from his ship if the trip was successful and a red one if it was not.

The distraught maiden waited one hundred days and finally spotted the prince's ship. What she saw, however, broke her heart—a red flag. She died from grief, thinking she would not be wed to the prince.

When the ship arrived in the harbor, the townspeople saw that the flag was really white but had been stained with the blood of the dragon that the prince had slain to regain the king's treasure. So although the prince was victorious in battle, he had lost in love. He returned in just enough time to attend his maiden's funeral. From her grave sprang the crape myrtle, which blooms for one hundred days each summer.

I look upon the whole country in springtime as a spacious garden, and make as many visits to a spot of daisies, or a bank of violets, as a florist does to his borders or parterres. There is not a bush in blossom within a mile of me which I am not acquainted with, nor scarce a daffodil or cowslip that withers away in my neighborhood without my missing it.

—JOSEPH ADDISON

MAGIC
Cynthia Panton

...

IN THE SPRING OF 1914, A YOUNG MAN NAMED Robert living in the small village of Surrey, England, asked a young woman named Margery to be his wife. Robert and Margery spent every waking moment together and were one of those couples whose passion was obvious even to strangers. All the villagers remarked on how deeply in love they were and everyone looked forward to their wedding.

In August of the same year, Great Britain declared war on Germany, and Robert, like so many other young men from his village, joined the Royal West Surrey Regiment. He and Margery vowed to marry in the summer of 1916, provided he could get a leave. While this time was difficult for them, their love and commitment to one another remained strong throughout their separation. They kept their sights locked on their future together, knowing that the wait was worth the reward.

On July 1, 1916, hundreds of British soldiers fought and died in the Battle of the Somme. Robert survived, always keeping his love for Margery and their future together before him. But in September 1916, Robert was killed. His body was never found.

Even though Margery eventually married someone else, she would never forget her Robbie. The engagement ring he gave her remained firmly on her finger until her death in 1968.

Margery's son David told me this story many years later, and I happily promised to put flowers on his mother's grave when I visited Surrey in the spring. After spending some time in the small village, I remembered my promise and walked to the florist shop. But to my dismay, a sign on the shop's door said that the florist was on holiday. Time was short, and I had no way of getting to another shop. I was upset that I wouldn't be able to leave flowers for this spirited woman who had loved her fiancé so deeply that she never let him go.

Surprisingly, the door of the shop stood ajar. I peeked in and saw two ladies chatting in the midst of dozens of elaborate hats. When I walked in, I was told that the florist shop doubled as a hat shop, and since there were two weddings in the village that afternoon the shop was open to women who'd ordered hats for the special occasions. There were no flowers in sight, but I asked the hat shop owner if it was possible to buy any flowers, sharing the story of Robbie and Margery with her. She said she was very sorry, but she was not the florist, and there weren't any flowers available. I thanked her, my hopes diminished, and had just turned to leave when I caught sight of something out of the corner of my eye. Lying on a side table was a large bouquet of fresh yellow carnations. My heart beat faster with excitement. Could these possibly be for sale? The hat shop owner could not explain where the flowers had come from; she had no idea why they were lying on the table by themselves, wrapped in paper as if waiting for a buyer.

I bought the flowers, and as I walked thoughtfully down the street with my bouquet of sunshine blooms something occurred to me: Perhaps these flowers had been left specifically and magically for me. Robbie could not let me leave the village without giving his one true love her flowers, a symbol of their eternal love.

AFRICAN VIOLETS (VIOLET *SAINTPAULIA* SERIES) ARE not true violets and are not hardy in temperate climates. They have fuzzy, heart-shaped leaves with light green or red-violet undersides. Some varieties may have variegated foliage that is ruffled, smooth, or have a serrated edge. Petals may be single, double, or ruffled. Colors include maroon, purple, violet, pink, yellow, white, red, blue, and bi-colors.

Keep the soil barely moist. Water directly to the root; water dripped on the leaves creates spotted foliage. Fertilize monthly with an all-purpose plant food. African violets flourish in bright, indirect sunlight. It is recommended to turn the plant every few weeks. They will do well in fourteen to sixteen hours of artificial light. They flower continuously and will last many years. Keep at 60 to 65 degrees Fahrenheit. They are sensitive to chill damage, so avoid drafts. Remove old blooms and yellowing leaves.

They will survive with benign neglect but will flourish with more attention.

GARNISHING A SALAD OR DESSERT WITH A scattering of edible flower petals or leaves makes an elegant presentation. Flowers also can be used to add subtle flavor or texture to a favorite recipe.

Marigolds and nasturtiums add a splash of bright color and a spicy flavor to a salad. Roses add a pretty garnish and subtle aroma to a feathery light mousse or pudding. Calendula has a buttery flavor, and pansies are minty.

A blend of violet blossoms and a few slivers of orange peel can be combined with a teaspoon of Darjeeling tea and tied in a six-inch square of muslin, then steeped in a teapot for four or five minutes to make a refreshing brew.

When using flowers in combination with food, be sure to use those that are unsprayed and healthy-looking. Wash the flower heads carefully because delicate flower petals bruise easily.

People from a planet without flowers
would think we must be mad with joy . . . to
have such things about us.

—IRIS MURDOCH

A LESSON IN APPRECIATION
Elisabeth Charles

. . .

I'VE ALWAYS BEEN A SUCKER FOR FLOWERS. MY husband, Curt, knew that I loved getting bouquets, and every now and then he would surprise me with one on a special occasion.

Curt and I had a commuter marriage when we started our lives together, so there were times when we would meet in the home of a relative in the city of our destination, rather than travel there together.

One year early in our marriage, I was coming home to the San Francisco Bay Area for the Christmas holidays on my birthday, December 17, to spend time with my family. Now, I have to admit that I'm a huge birthday person and love to have a big fuss made over me. Curt had told me that my birthday gift would be waiting upon my arrival. I couldn't wait to get to my parents' house to see what he had sent me—only to learn that there was a dozen roses, but nothing else.

When I found out that all he had sent was flowers, I

immediately called him to berate him. I told him that sending flowers was a no-brainer and asked where was my real birthday present.

Well, he did not take kindly to that at all. He said that if flowers were such a no-brainer, then obviously I wouldn't miss getting them for the next several years. And true to his word, he refused to send me flowers for the next three years! Try as I might to break the moratorium, he would remind me of how rudely I had rejected his last bouquet and would say that I didn't deserve flowers.

I was absolutely crushed, but I have to admit that my scoldings were well deserved. I can't remember what momentous occasion broke the stalemate, but it had to be something pretty big, because now once in a blue moon he'll send me flowers. He knows he doesn't have to worry about my not appreciating them. Needless to say, I've never made another rude or unkind, unappreciative comment about any gift he's ever given me. I know better! You never know how precious something is until it is taken away. I learned that lesson the hard way.

chapter three

Beginning Steps

EVERY BLADE OF GRASS, EACH LEAF,

EACH SEPARATE FLORET AND PETAL,

IS AN INSCRIPTION SPEAKING OF HOPE.

—*Richard Jeffries*

WINDOW SHOPPING
Craig Sole

· · ·

DURING WEDDING CONSULTATIONS, I FRE-
quently ask couples how they became engaged. The stories
always give me a better sense of who the people are and what
kinds of flowers will best suit them. I've heard many stories,
from the wildly romantic to the traditional. Each story has its
own unique twist, just as each couple has its own identity.
One of the most romantic proposals I've heard came from
Scott and Jennifer.

On the day he planned to propose, Scott invited Jennifer
and his parents to his favorite little trendy restaurant in
Kansas City, where they all lived. But what Jennifer believed
was just a simple get-together would turn out to be a day that
none of them would forget. Next door to the restaurant was
a jewelry store where the couple had window-shopped many
times, the very jewelry store where Jennifer had seen and long
admired a stunning engagement ring. Arriving early for lunch,
Scott and Jennifer walked slowly past the display. Suspended
in the window was a lovely bouquet of garden flowers.
Jennifer commented that this was exactly the kind of bouquet
she would want if she were getting married, made up of all the
spring colors and flowers like the ones in her grandmother's
garden. With his parents watching from across the street, the
employees of the jewelry store looking on through darkened

windows, and the noon lunch crowd observing from all sides, Scott knelt down on one knee and proposed to Jennifer.

Only after her enthusiastic response did she notice the ring that she loved so much nestled in the center of the flower bouquet, and the scroll of parchment placed neatly alongside the arrangement with the words "Jennifer, will you marry me?" in Spencerian script. That was when she realized that this moment had been designed for her—as was this wonderful man.

SOME FLOWERING AND FOLIAGE PLANTS CAN add fresh air to a home environment by removing pollutants such as benzene, formaldehyde, xylene, toluene, and trichloroethylene.

Studies have shown that just two potted plants per hundred square feet of floor space will help clean and refresh the air.

Azaleas, chrysanthemums, and poinsettias are effective air cleaners for formaldehyde emitted from carpeting, clothes, furniture, foam insulation, household cleaners, paper goods, particleboard, plywood, and water repellants.

Chrysanthemums, gerbera daisies, and peace lilies work well to clean the air of benzene and trichloroethylene emitted from detergents, gasoline, inks, oils, plastics, synthetic fibers, tobacco smoke, adhesives, dry cleaning, lacquers, paints, and varnishes.

QUEEN VICTORIA'S WEDDING BOUQUET WAS filled with myrtle, a plant material not commonly seen at that point in history. After the wedding the myrtle was planted on the grounds of the palace, and it grew into a beautiful, abundant bush. From that day to this, every British royal bride carries a piece of myrtle in her bouquet.

IN GREEK MYTHOLOGY, A NYMPH, ECHO, WAS infatuated by a handsome youth, Narcissus. He rejected her, saying that he cared for no woman's love. Echo was upset and enlisted the help of Cupid. If she couldn't have him, she didn't want anyone to have him. Cupid caused Narcissus to fall in love with his own image in a reflecting pool. His love was unrequited, and he wasted away alongside the pool. While the nymphs prepared his funeral pyre, his body was transformed into the flower we now call narcissus.

*Those who contemplate the beauty of the earth
find reserves of strength that will endure as
long as life lasts. There is symbolic as well as
actual beauty in the migration of the birds,
the ebb and flow of the tides, the folded bud
for the spring. There is something infinitely
healing in the repeated refrains of nature—
the assurance that dawn comes after night,
and spring after the winter.*

—Rachel Carson

Mystery at Storm Lake
Barbara Glanz

. . .

When I think about the way my parents met, I wonder what would have become of me had my mother not been a flower lover.

When my mother, Lucille Anderson, graduated from college, she earned a prized position as the art teacher in Storm Lake, Iowa. In small towns like Storm Lake, the pictures of new teachers are published in the local newspaper every summer, welcoming them to the community. And so, that August, my mother's picture was published with the rest.

My father, Wayne Bauerle, was a successful and single young man working for Standard Oil. He was a quiet man, but very determined, and when he spoke, people listened. He saw my mother's picture and decided right then that he was going to marry her, so he devised a romantic strategy.

My father took careful steps, first by discovering my mother's address and then by sending her a bouquet of flowers—every day for the next two weeks. Imagine receiving flowers every day for two weeks from a perfect stranger! Finally, my mother's landlady called my father and told him that if he sent any more flowers he'd have to send along more vases. My mother said the place looked like a funeral parlor! My dad was pretty shrewd, waiting all that time before asking my mom for a date. How could this woman, he mused, possibly turn him down after all those flowers?

She couldn't, and she didn't. They met, went out, fell in love, got married, had four children, and remained hopelessly romantic until my father passed away. And my sentimental father made sure that my mother had fresh flowers in our home every week of their marriage.

THE WAX BEGONIA PLANT *(BEGONIA SEMPER-florens)* has close-clustered single or double flowers in shades of red, pink, peach, or white. It is commonly used as a bedding plant. The plant's stout stems are succulent, with lots of branches containing shiny, heart-shaped green, bronze, or mottled leaves. Plants grow from six to twelve inches tall and from six to twelve inches wide.

Plant wax begonias in partial shade outdoors; provide maximum light when growing them indoors. Keep the soil moist but not wet—yellowing lower leaves and drooping plants are signs that the soil is too wet. Root rot will occur if the plant is overwatered. Avoid temperatures above 75 degrees Fahrenheit and below 55 degrees Fahrenheit.

These plants do best in fertile, well-drained soil when planted outdoors. Plants may be dug up before the first frost and used as houseplants.

PLASTIC SLEEVES DESIGNED FOR SLIDES ARE perfect for tracking plants or harvesting seeds. These sleeves fit a standard three-ring binder. The see-through pockets are also perfect for pressed flowers and clippings.

HEALING YARROW (ACHILLEA SPP.) LIGHTS UP a summer herb garden with its brilliant gold, white, and pastel blooms. Butterflies love yarrow.

According to legend, Achilles used it to stanch the bleeding wounds of his soldiers. The plant contains chemicals that cause the blood to coagulate, along with other chemicals that help to relieve pain and inflammation and prevent infection.

DRIED LAVENDER BUDS OR ROSE PETALS USED on their own or in combination with other dried flowers and spices can be used to fill a pincushion instead of batting, stuffing, or sand. Each time a pin is inserted, a hint of subtle fragrance is emitted.

To see a World in a Grain of Sand
And a heaven in a Wild Flower,
Hold infinity in the palm of your hand
And Eternity in an hour.

—WILLIAM BLAKE

FLIGHT OF FANCY
Nada Rutka

...

WHEN MY HUSBAND, STEPHEN, AND I WERE dating, he frequently met me at the airport with flowers. We had a commuter relationship. I lived in Pittsburgh, Pennsylvania, and he lived in Raleigh, North Carolina. Seeing each other only two or three times a month was difficult, but our times together were wonderful. My business travels allowed me to connect many of my weekends to business trips to North Carolina. As I would get off the plane, seeing Stephen standing there with flowers in his hands, the lost time would be immediately forgotten.

We had been dating for eleven months after accidentally meeting through mutual friends. Usually, when I was making a visit, we didn't bother to make plans; instead, we were spontaneous and played it by ear. But one particular trip was different. Stephen called to tell me that we were going to go straight from the airport to a fancy restaurant. I was curious, but very excited. I wasn't sure, of course, but I had a feeling that that might be the night he would propose.

When we were seated at the restaurant, Stephen ordered a bottle of the best champagne, and within moments the maitre d' approached the table carrying a dozen of the largest, most beautiful South American red roses for me. The whole event had been carefully prearranged. Before I could say anything, Stephen proposed. We were married five months later, on the second of February.

During the first year of our marriage, I received roses on the second day of each month totaling the number of months we had been married. I found the flowers in a new place every time: sometimes at work, sometimes at home, sometimes at a restaurant where we were dining, and sometimes within our house or yard. One time he placed them in front of the door leading from the garage, and another time they were hidden in the downstairs refrigerator—I found them only after he asked me to grab him a beer.

We have been married fifteen years, and now I grow roses of my own: Audrey Hepburns (my favorite), Mr. Lincolns, and Georgia. Voluminous red roses bloom just outside my office window, and I have nine or ten bushes in my own yard. The flowers fill the rooms in our house, reminding me of our beginnings and how lucky Stephen and I are to have each other. Oh, I still receive the occasional "just because" bouquets, and even though there aren't any hidden flowers to be found anymore, I have found that our lives together keep getting better, richer, and fuller.

LONG BEFORE THERE WAS A VALENTINE'S DAY, PEO-
ple linked the beauty and fragrance of flowers
with ideas of love and romance. The Greeks and
Romans had a love story for almost every kind of
flower. In one myth, Cupid hurries off to a council of the gods on Mount Olympus carrying a vase
of nectar for them to drink. He stumbles and
spills the nectar, and it bubbles up from the
earth in the form of roses.

FOR A SPECIAL CELEBRATION, CREATE AN ALL-ROSE
bouquet. The visual effect and the scent will be
intoxicating. Combine stems of hybrid tea roses,
voluptuous garden roses, and spray roses with
daintier sweetheart or miniature roses. Choose
roses of analogous colors (colors close to each
other on the color wheel): peach, yellow, and
pale pink or cream; or champagne and blush
pink. Lavender, deep rose, and hot pink is another good combination.

In this world we walk on hell's roof
and gaze at flowers.

—ISSA

THE FLIGHT OF THE HELICOPTER
Shirley Sluis

. . .

YEARS AGO, WHEN MY SISTER AND I OPENED A
flower shop called Flowers by Shir Laine, we quickly became
aware of the emotions that flowers evoke. We learned that
sometimes the emotions felt by a person when receiving a floral gift resurface long after the flowers are gone. One story in
particular sticks in my mind.

A young woman came into our shop and asked if we
could make a helicopter out of flowers. All we knew was that
she was very much in love with a pilot who would be leaving
for duty soon. She wanted him to know her feelings before he
left, and had decided that this unique flower creation would
be the perfect way to do it. We made the display, which turned
out beautifully, and sent it off to her true love. Before we sent
it, we took a snapshot because we liked to exhibit our "special" creations on the cooler wall so that other customers
could take a look. We never heard anything more from the
young woman, and hoped that the flowers had the desired
effect.

Many years later, a man came into our shop with two small children. He guided them to the cooler wall and pointed out the picture of the helicopter arrangement. When I asked if there was something I could help him with, he said no, he was just showing his children the flowers that their mother had sent to him when they were going together. I was thrilled to finally know what had happened to the young woman and her pilot—and that the flowers had done the trick!

IF A ROSE WILTS PREMATURELY IT USUALLY MEANS the end of the stem is clogged with bacteria or an air pocket has formed. The rose is unable to drink water. Simply recut the stem about one inch from the end and submerge the whole rose in warm water till it revives.

ACCORDING TO AN OLD ENGLISH LEGEND, A ROSE can help a young girl find a husband. In Victorian times, husbands used small rose bouquets called tussie-mussies to communicate devotion, trust, and love. An anniversary tussie-mussie today could contain the number of red roses representing the months or years a couple has spent sharing happy moments together.

GUERNSEY LILY (*NERINE SARNIENSIS*) IS THE NAME given to thirty species of amaryllis-like plants that have strap-shaped leaves and beautiful white, pink, or red flowers. All the species are native to southern Africa. According to legend, the Guernsey lily first appeared on the island of Guernsey when a fairy king won the hand and heart of a beautiful maiden named Michelle. When he tried to take her away to his kingdom, she protested, saying that she didn't want to leave her family. She begged the king to give her a token by which her family could remember her always. The king gave her the bulb of a lily. Michelle planted the bulb, and it burst into flower after she left Guernsey. When her mother went looking for Michelle and saw the lily, she immediately knew it was from her daughter and understood the message that she would never see Michelle again.

THE FLOWERS OF THE BRILLIANT RED HIBISCUS native to Hawaii (*Hibiscus kokio*) were worn by men to send messages to women. Worn behind the right ear, they meant "I am married"; behind the left ear, "I am single and looking for a lover." If a flower was worn behind both ears the message was clear: "I am married, but looking for another lover."

FRESH CUT ROSES DISPLAY BEST IN VASES THAT ARE about half as tall as the flowers; for example, an eighteen-inch-tall rose looks best in a nine-inch-tall vase.

TO GIVE A SIMPLE BUD VASE ARRANGEMENT A FIN-ished look, tuck a few small leaves at the rim and tie a pretty ribbon around the neck of the vase.

TRY FLOATING JUST ONE OR TWO GARDEN ROSES IN a crystal bowl full of water for a spectacular display.

HYBRID TEA ROSES HAVE LARGE FLOWERS. THE FIRST, La France, was bred in 1867 by Jean-Baptiste Guillot.

THE MOST IMPORTANT WINDOW PLANT IN WINTER IS the amaryllis, which belongs to a family of flowering bulbs containing more than seventy varieties. If the bulb is a gift, it will probably come already planted in a container with directions on the package. Follow the instructions on the package for the first year. Repot the bulb during the autumn that follows blooming, after the leaves begin to turn yellow and die back.

If the bulb isn't already planted, plant it in a soil mix of a third each potting soil, sharp sand, and composted manure. Place the bulb halfway into a pot that is no more than two inches larger in diameter than the bulb. Leave the top part of the bulb uncovered. The soil should be kept moist but not wet. When the bulb begins to sprout, it should have at least four hours or more of full sun in a temperature of at least 50 degrees Fahrenheit at night and 70 degrees Fahrenheit during the day.

Replace the top inch of soil with fresh potting mix every year, and replace the pot every three years. Over time, a healthy bulb can produce many flowers and get to be fourteen inches in diameter.

The amaryllis should be allowed to rest in a cool, dry, dark place from late October to mid-December. When you want the plant to bloom, bring the pot into a warm room and place it in a dim or dark spot. The flower stalk will begin to emerge, and when it is six inches tall, place the plant in a sunny window.

A rose has no why or wherefore; it blooms
because it blooms, has no concerns outside of
itself and doesn't seek to be seen.

—ANGELUS SILESIUS

PLAYING MY PART
Alice-Lynne Olson

. . .

AS A WEDDING FLORIST, I HAVE HAD THE opportunity to meet some wonderful people over the years. And though many of the faces and names have become a blur, certain people left a lasting impression, people I will never forget. And so it was with Dean and Jennifer.

About five years ago, I was managing a flower shop in Bloomington, Minnesota. Dean was a handsome young man who was courting a pretty young lady named Jennifer, whom he'd met while doing missionary work abroad. They were both from Minnesota, but she lived about an hour away in Minneapolis. Somehow he found my shop and me, and what began as a bouquet of daisies and carnations evolved into a three-year courtship. During that time, Dean bought from me every flower Jennifer got. He sent her flowers on birthdays, anniversaries, her mother's birthday, her dog's birthday, and any other occasion he could use as an excuse.

Into the third year of this courtship, Dean confided in me

that he was going to propose to Jennifer while they were on a mission trip to Egypt later that spring. I was leaving my retail job soon to start my own business, so I gave him my phone number and asked him to keep me posted. Not long after this conversation with Dean I opened my own design studio. I occasionally thought about Dean and Jennifer and wondered if I would ever hear from them. And then one day, I did! Dean called and told me that he had lost my phone number. He eventually turned to the Internet and tracked me down. He and Jennifer had been engaged for months, but they had put off setting a date until they found me to do their wedding flowers. Because I had played such an integral part in their courtship and romance, he explained, it was unthinkable for any other florist to do the job. I was excited and flattered. And so the planning began.

It was a huge wedding: eight attendants, four flower girls, and guests from all over the world. As the flower girls walked down the aisle, they gently tossed rose petals from their baskets on either side of the bride's path to the altar. But there was something special about the petals in their baskets: Jennifer had saved every flower that Dean had ever given her, and these were the petals she walked on to meet her true love. This beautiful story was included in their wedding program, where they also made a point of mentioning my important role in their relationship.

I learned something from Dean and Jennifer: If you are truly passionate about what you do, it shows in every petal of every flower that leaves your hands and finds it way into the hands of a nervous, smiling bride. This couple, so much in love, reminded me why I had decided to devote my life to making beautiful and lasting floral wedding memories. I was reminded, too, of the important role that flowers play in courtship, romance, and marriage.

GETTING YOUR GARDEN IN SHAPE

- Prepare a new bed by digging the area a foot deep. Turn the grass you remove upside down and put grass clippings on top of the first layer of soil. Add the rest of the soil that has been removed and wait a season or two before planting.
- Keep a photographic record of what is blooming, then review the pictures. This allows relocating plants next to each other for the best mix of color. The best time to move plants is spring or fall, and they might not be blooming then.
- Increase enjoyment of the garden by having some of the photos made into calendars. Give these calendars as holiday gifts.
- Grow flowers to dry. Use them to decorate miniature grapevine wreaths and fill clear plastic tree ornaments. Decorate a Christmas tree with your creations or give them as gifts.
- Work out and lift weights to keep in shape for heavy gardening chores that need to be done.

> **When I place a flower on my night table and
> sketch it faithfully it seems to me that, little
> by little, I comprehend the secret of creation.**
>
> —SHIKI

TWELVE DAYS OF CHRISTMAS
Janice Stucky

. . .

MY HUSBAND, DAVE, AND I WERE MARRIED ON
December 12. Due to our job commitments, we couldn't go
on a honeymoon until after the first of the year, yet we decided to get married anyway. We couldn't wait to be together for
the rest of our lives. Dave is a true romantic and wanted to
start our lives together in a special way—even if we couldn't
do it through the excitement of an actual honeymoon. Unknown to me, he teamed up with our local florist, and the day
after our wedding the floral surprises began.

The doorbell rang shortly after I returned home from
work. There stood a deliveryman holding a magnificent poinsettia plant with a single blooming red flower. The attached
card said, "I pledge my love to you." I was impressed and feeling very warm about the beginning of our new life together.
When Dave got home that night, he saw the plant sitting on
the kitchen table in our small apartment and smiled from ear
to ear. I ran up to him and gave him a big hug and kiss.

The next day, around the same time, the doorbell sounded again. The same deliveryman stood there smiling as he held out a wrapped package. I thanked him and went inside. Upon opening the package, I found two large white gardenias floating in a clear bowl of water. The attached note said, "On this second day of our lives together, I promise to hold you like a tender flower forever." Wow! This was really cool, I thought. Dave had a cute little smirk on his face when he got home that night. I loved it.

Well, the tradition continued. Every evening for the next nine days I received flowers from the same florist, delivered by the same deliveryman. There were three yellow orchids, then four long-stemmed peach roses, five pink carnations, six fragrant purple freesia, seven blue asters, eight yellow mums, nine pink lilies, ten purple gladiolas, and eleven white daisies. With each delivery came a creatively worded note from Dave that told me of his love and devotion while referring to the number of days we had been married. I started looking forward to each day's delivery, trying to guess what kind of flower would arrive. All of my friends at work were getting involved as they looked forward to hearing my daily story. On Christmas Eve, the last delivery was made. Up the walk came my new friend Tim, the floral deliveryman. By this time, we were on a first-name basis, chatting about everything from the weather to what he and his family were doing for Christmas to what this day's delivery might contain. Tim was holding a large wrapped bouquet in his arms. Holding it out to me, he said that he had never been part of such a showing of love, and he wished us a long, loving life together as husband and wife. Running back inside with my flowers, I opened the paper to find twelve beautiful long-stemmed red roses with a note that said, "These roses are for the first twelve days of our married life, the twelve days of Christmas, and to celebrate the beginning of forever together, I love you." Who needed a honeymoon after that!

It's been twenty-nine years since our first Christmas together. We did go on our honeymoon to Florida after the first of the year, as planned, but it was almost anticlimactic compared to the excitement of the first twelve days of our marriage.

Now, with three grown children, we sometimes reminisce about Dave's plan and how important it was to me as we started our lives together. I carefully saved each and every note, placing them in a specially created album along with photos of each day's gift of flowers. During some of the low times in our lives together, I have simply pulled out this album. It never ceases to remind me of Dave's love and his desire to please me. The flowers themselves are long gone, but the memory of them is so strong it has lasted through twenty-nine years of marriage.

POINSETTIAS ARE SOMETIMES CALLED CHRISTMAS stars or Flor de Noche Buena, and truly symbolize Christmas to Americans more than any other single plant. The genus is *Euphorbia,* and they are available in red, white, and pink.

What we think of as the colorful petals of the poinsettia are really specialized, modified leaves called bracts. The true flowers are the tiny yellow balls clustered in the center of the bracts. Some are male and some are female. The flower tips often exude small beads of crystal-clear nectar.

Poinsettias have a white, milky sap, called latex. Although this sap has been blamed for causing effects ranging from dermatitis all the way to death in children and pets, recent findings refute this.

Care and handling of the poinsettia plant will ensure a very long life and sizable growth as a houseplant. On receiving the plant, remove the foil wrap. The pot will be full of roots, so special care should be taken to water all of the soil, not just the uppermost layer. Large concentrations of peat moss in the soil are common and can dry quickly in the warm air of heated homes. If the plant begins to wilt, soak it, pot and all, in a bucket of water. Keep the plant at around 65 degrees Fahrenheit and away from cool drafts.

Poinsettias are short-day plants. If you want them to blossom again, they shouldn't receive more than twelve hours of light starting October 1. To simulate this, the plant can be covered with black cloth or placed under a box for the appropriate time. After the plant starts to bud, the blackouts are no longer needed.

One of the buds on the rosebush opened into a blossom, white and silky as a baby's fist.

—NATALIE BABBIT

TRADING FOR MEMORIES OF LOVE
Lynn Downing

...

SINCE 1996, NOVEMBER 3 REMINDS ME OF A beautiful four-letter word that begins with *r*—*rose*. It has not always been that way.

There is another four-letter word beginning with *r* that all too many women have painfully experienced. That word is *rape*. In 1992, as a freshman in college, that word became a reality to me as I was raped by a guy who lived a floor below me in the dorm. The date was November 3.

It was a day I had been looking forward to—my first Election Day. Having turned eighteen, I was now old enough to vote. Although most people don't really remember the first time they voted, because of the rape it was nearly impossible for me to forget. As November 3 rolled around each year I experienced an "anniversary" reaction, struggling with memories I desperately wanted to erase. It sent me into a bout of depression.

Then I met Blaine. We began dating in the fall of 1996. As we neared November 3, I confided to him what had happened and warned him about my recurring reaction. His response was simple and straightforward: "Well, we'll just have to make a happy memory for that day."

I was living with my parents at the time, having graduated from college earlier that year. Blaine and I were having a long-distance romance since we lived four hundred miles apart. I had forgotten his offhanded comment. And then, on November 3, as I was toweling off from a shower, the doorbell rang. My mom answered and excitedly called to me. She was crying as she walked into the bathroom holding a breathtakingly beautiful bouquet of roses—a gift of a new beginning for me.

The flowers were sent by the man I had recently begun dating, the man who would one day be my husband. This was the one and only time he has ever sent me flowers. We now lovingly joke together that November 3 was *the* day he sent me flowers. However, those roses were more important to me on that particular day than dozens of roses arriving regularly ever could be. Nothing can take away from the power of that gift.

November 3 still reminds me of a four-letter word that begins with *r*. But I've traded reliving a rape for reliving those roses. I realize that bad memories are never completely forgotten, but gradually the rape is fading into the background as the beauty and fragrance of that very special bouquet of roses live so brightly in the foreground of my memories of my husband and his love.

UNEXPECTED FLOWERS ARE THE MOST PLEASING gifts. In a world that often reminds us of days to remember each other, I find the days we create ourselves are the ones that create the most profound impact psychologically.

THE LANGUAGE OF FLOWERS SUGGESTS THAT IVY represents fidelity, marriage, and friendship. New sprigs of growth mean "I am eager to please." Victorians bought friendship brooches showing ivy clinging around a tree with inscriptions in English or Latin that said "Nothing can detach me from you."

Alexei Tolstoy compared the strength of ivy with the strength of love in *Crimean Sketches* (ca. 1857):

> *But now young ivy, twining round*
> *Its walls, war's traces has concealed.*
> *Has my love not yet likewise wound*
> *Around your wounds, have they not yet*
> *   healed?*

FREESIA IS GROWN FROM CORMS, WHICH ARE BULB-like structures that resemble small onions. It is one of the most fragrant flowers available and can be found in numerous colors.

Freesia is native to the Cape Province of South Africa and is named after the German physician Friedrich Freese, a student of South African plants. It is especially useful when placed in a vase that receives slight air movement such as near a window or in a pathway where people often pass. This airflow moves the fragrance into the room and can be intoxicatingly beautiful.

*Arranging a bowl of flowers in the morning
can give a sense of quiet in a crowded day—
like writing a poem, or saying a prayer.*

—ANNE MORROW LINDBERGH

THE PROMISE OF ROSES
Carolina Fernandez
. . .

THE FIRST TIME I SAW HIM, HE WAS WALKING
in the parking lot of the IBM office where I was interviewing
for the third time. With a newly acquired M.B.A., I was ready
to nail the interview and land the job, but I was now clearly
distracted. His suit jacket was slung over his shoulder, casually but certainly not arrogantly. His walk was confident. He
was tall, dark, and handsome, even at fifty yards away.

When I was invited back for the fourth and final interview, I noticed him sitting at a desk. *He must work here!* I
screamed to myself, now extremely distracted as I walked into
the interview of my life.

I got the offer, which included, along with travel perks and
other luxuries, more money than my grad-school brain could
comprehend. My excitement was uncontainable. I walked out
of that office as if on a cloud. I simply had to announce my
news to someone! Ahh . . . there he was. I would tell him! I
determined on the spot to be instantly cool and funny and

smart all at once, but all I could muster, as his eyes met mine, was a soft "Hi." But I did notice that up close he was even more gorgeous than he was from fifty yards away.

My job was scheduled to start in five months, so I planned to relax, travel, and enjoy myself before my working life officially started. This plan was short-lived, however. A few days later I received a phone call from the IBM branch manager, who asked if I would help them out and fill a temporary switchboard operator position until my real job started.

"Me? Work the switchboard?" I fumbled some lame response and politely refused the offer. My arrogant twenty-something mind was thinking: *You've got to be joking. An M.B.A. at a switchboard answering phones all day? I'm going to travel. Maybe go to Europe for a while.*

My widowed mother—yes, the same mom who financed not only my four-year private college education but my two-year graduate education—was standing in my kitchen when I took that call.

I explained that the company wanted me to temporarily work the switchboard. Humph. "Forget it," I told her. "I'm going to Europe."

"On what?" Mom asked.

"Oh, I don't know. MasterCard probably."

"Honey, I hate to tell you, but your Sugar Mama is tired. Forget Europe. You're taking that job!"

It took me a while to regain my composure, not to mention a healthy dose of humility, but a couple of hours later I called and accepted the temporary job. I started work the following Tuesday.

To my surprise, that very first morning "he" walked up to the switchboard and introduced himself. His name was Ernie Fernandez. He was Latin, born in Cuba and raised in Lexington, Kentucky, from the age of three. He was as American as apple pie, with the impeccable manners befitting a true Southern gentleman. I was quick to point out that this switchboard thing was strictly temporary and that my "real" position would start in January. It didn't seem to matter to him. He was happy just to stop by during the day to chat and to see if I needed a cool glass of water or a cup of coffee to break the monotony of answering phone lines.

After work that first night the entire office was hosting a going-away party at a nearby restaurant for a marketing rep I had not yet met. Through Ernie's invitation I found myself not just attending the party but staying for dinner with several other IBMers. Ernie invited me to spend the evening in a chair right next to him. I *graciously* agreed.

When I returned home to my one-bedroom apartment, my faithful dog, Misha, was eager to hear about my first day at the ole switchboard. She listened to all the boring details, but her ears really perked up when I told her about Ernie. In fact, Misha was the first to hear that this was the guy I wanted to marry.

I was falling, and I was falling hard, fast, and deep. On Friday afternoon, a beautiful woman walked into the office, came up to my switchboard, and asked to see Ernie. He strolled out, embraced her, and gave her a kiss. A warm kiss. My heart sank. I should have known. Someone as wonderful as he would of course be spoken for.

The next Friday afternoon, when everyone was making plans to leave for the weekend, Ernie came up to my desk and asked me out for the next afternoon. On a real date at last, we enjoyed an open-air concert in the park, and then I invited him to the gym to join me in a swim. An avid lap swimmer to this day, I have always taken my daily swims seriously, and I was curious to see the stuff this guy was really made of. To my surprise, he not only went to the gym with me, he actually got into the pool and swam laps with me—without goggles, bless his heart—for the first hour. That was the clincher. His blood-shot eyes begged for mercy, and my heart was sealed.

A long dinner on Sunday led to a walk with Misha. It was on this walk that I learned that the gorgeous woman in the lobby was Ernie's kid sister. What a relief!

We couldn't seem to stay away from each other and spent several hours together Monday as well.

Ernie rang my doorbell Wednesday night with a dozen long-stemmed red roses in his right hand and dinner for two in his left. He set it all down, swept me up in his arms, and asked me to marry him. Then. There. Four days after our first date. I said yes.

It's hard to believe that we both could have been so compulsive at twenty-four years of age, and we remain completely mortified at the thought that one of our four children would ever do the same thing. For even though we waited three months to tell anyone other than our family and a full nine months from that first date to have a large and formal church wedding, we still acted on a compulsion that would strike instant panic in our hearts if our kids did anything even close.

But those first red roses are safely tucked away, along with the dozen long-stemmed white roses from our wedding day, and the fifteen from the day Nicolas was born, the fourteen from the day Benjamin was born, the twelve from the birth of Cristina, and the whopping twenty-five from Victor's day of birth. Roses will always be my flower. They have been from that Wednesday night when my wonderful Ernie carried them into my tiny apartment with dinner and a proposal.

chapter four

Withstanding the Test of Time

LET BOTH GROW TOGETHER
UNTIL THE HARVEST.

— Matthew 13:30

Throughout Our Garden
Tim Farrell

...

🎗 "Look what I picked for Mommy," said Katie as she scampered across the yard with a fistful of pink tulips. "They're so soft and pretty. I just know she'll love them." Smiling and stopping only long enough to kiss my cheek, my little five-year-old princess headed for the house to present her mother these gathered treasures.

"Soft and pretty." Her words dangled in the air as if waiting for a response. Funny, the way flowers mean different things to different people. As my daughter approached me with the tulips I had been thinking something other than "soft and pretty"; to me, pink tulips have been the epitome of bravery and strength for more than five years.

My mind takes me back to the autumn of 1993. My wife, Bernadette, and I were busy planting tulip bulbs, hundreds of them, throughout our garden. We had just found out that Bernadette was carrying our third child. Already blessed with two sons, we were thrilled with the news of our newest arrival, due in May. While shopping at a garden center that week, we both agreed to follow our instincts and fill our cart with pink tulip bulbs. We just knew we were going to have a girl.

Just a few weeks later, the weather changed. It was the beginning of a long, cold winter. Just as suddenly as the weather

changed, so had Bernadette's health. It was the beginning of
a long, difficult pregnancy. She was diagnosed with a severe
case of hyperemesis, which is a condition that made her
unable to keep down any food or liquid. By late October, she
had already been hospitalized four times, her longest stay
being almost two weeks. She had dehydrated several times,
needing intravenous fluids. Her body weakened and her condition became more fragile. Eventually, the doctors had to
insert a central line in order to provide some kind of nutrition
for her and the baby. For more than twelve weeks, I could do
nothing but watch as my wife lay helplessly attached to an IV
pump, every hour of every day. My own helplessness was sur-
passed only by my admiration for Bernadette's strength and
courage.

It was shortly after welcoming the new year that the tubes
and machines were gone. By early spring, Bernadette was feeling much better, and her doctor assured us that the baby was
growing beautifully, despite all of the difficulties.

Then one April morning I noticed something. Throughout our garden, just breaking the ground, were clusters and
clusters of tulip sprouts. The sight brought tears to my eyes.
Just as Bernadette had endured her own harsh winter, so had
the tulips. Somehow they had managed to survive the bitter
cold, without the nutrition of the sun, without even an occasional watering. But there they were, just like my wife, awaiting the promise of spring.

A few weeks later, those strong, brave tulips colored
our garden a magnificent shade of pink. And I was there to
admire their beauty. Yes, I was there with my strong, brave

wife, our two sons, and our healthy and beautiful newborn daughter.

So you see, tulips *are* soft and pretty. They are also brave and strong. And although flowers themselves might not have souls, they certainly remind us of the wonderful qualities that are within those we love.

TULIPS LOVE THE SUN AND WILL STRETCH their heads to face the closest light source. They continue to grow even after being cut, which is why they often seem out of place a day after having been inserted into an arrangement.

When bringing home purchased tulips, allow them to remain in the plastic sleeve they are displayed in. While they are still wrapped in the sleeve, trim half an inch off the bottom of each stem with a floral knife or floral shears and place the entire bunch in cool, clean water for about four hours. Remove the sleeve after this time.

For long-lasting tulips, remove them every few days from their vase, wash the vase, recut the stems, and return the tulips to the vase, now filled with fresh water and floral preservative.

Oh, were my love yon lilac fair
Wi' purple blossoms to the spring,
And I a bird to shelter there,
When wearied on my little wing.

—ROBERT BURNS

LILACS: TO HAVE AND TO HOLD
Kathy Baker

. . .

MY HUSBAND, PHIL, GAVE ME FOUR SMALL lilac bushes for my birthday in 1993. Such an ordinary gift, but one that represented a promise fulfilled . . . and a gift of hope for the future.

Lilacs are very special to me; they remind me of my mother, who passed away a number of years ago. Many trees, flowers, plants, and lilac bushes surrounded the house where I grew up. The lilacs are what I remember most—that sweet, rich fragrance and the plump purple and white clusters. Just the smell of lilacs carries me home again. I remember taking huge bouquets of lilacs to school in honor of the Virgin Mary each May; I remember my mother making generous clusters for us to carry to our neighbors each spring; and I remember sitting near the lilac bushes, drinking in their delicious scent as I played in the grass. To me, lilacs have always symbolized the innocence of childhood and the bountiful beauty of springtime. But now, because of Phil's gift, lilacs mean so much more.

In 1992, less than three months before my birthday, we moved into a new house. One winter day, as we walked around our new backyard, making plans to fill in the empty lawn with trees and shrubs, I mentioned to Phil that I would like to get some lilac bushes to plant in the spring. That was one of the last "normal" conversations my husband and I would have for quite some time. Phil was diagnosed with multiple myeloma, an incurable cancer of the bone marrow, just a few weeks later.

Our lives were forever changed. Following diagnosis, Phil was hospitalized for nearly six weeks while undergoing orthopedic surgery and other treatments. When he came home, he was frail and weak, wearing a back brace and using a walker. I had nearly forgotten about my approaching birthday, but our children had gotten a cake and invited a few friends over. Phil was dressed in an old flannel shirt and a pair of baggy sweatpants, looking like a shadow of his former self. He was still in the process of getting over the surgery—and accepting the diagnosis. He was also facing extensive chemotherapy.

As you can imagine, I was not expecting anything from Phil for my birthday. I was brought to tears, though, as he made his way over to me with his walker clutching a small, unwrapped jewelry box, and placed the box on the table in front of me. Lifting the box, and feeling its weight, I knew it didn't contain jewelry. It was probably the only box Phil could find on the spur of the moment. Opening the box, I found a small, hand-scribbled note that simply said "4 lilac bushes." I looked at him with a questioning look. He said that his gift would be a little delayed and that he would have it for me as soon as he was strong enough to go get it. His present, he told me, was four small lilacs to represent each of our four children. Some weeks later, with the help of our friend John, Phil went to the nursery and picked out the plants, which John then planted for us in the backyard.

As I write this, my eyes are filled with tears just thinking about Phil's precious gift. Some women receive diamonds, cruises, or expensive works of art as gifts from their husbands; very nice, I'm sure, but not nearly as priceless as Phil's gift to me. He gave me what I most wanted that day: hope for the future and a promise that we will live each day together as fully as possible, for as long as possible. This is, after all, what we promised each other on our wedding day.

The beauty of the story is yet untold. Phil has beaten all of the medical odds—not just surviving, but thriving. He is now back to work, teaching part-time, and the lilac bushes in our backyard are a daily reminder of Phil's love . . . and a promise kept.

LILACS ARE NATIVE TO EUROPE AND THE TEMPERATE zones of Asia. They are popular spring flowers, prized for their delicate blooms and intoxicating fragrance. Lilacs are members of the Oleaceae, or olive, family. Their genus name is *Syringa,* derived from the Greek *syrinx,* or "pipe," which refers to the flower's hollow shoots. The blooms are available in a variety of shades, including white, lavender, blue, and purple-red.

Proper hydration is the key to maximizing vase life. After cutting flowers from the bush, submerge the lilac cuttings in fresh water and cut two to three inches from the branch ends. Do not split or pound lilac branches, since these procedures damage the branches' water transport structures.

ACCORDING TO THE LANGUAGE OF FLOWERS, the white lilac symbolizes purity, modesty, and youthful innocence. The purple lilac suggests the first emotions of love.

I believe a leaf of grass is no less than
the journey-work of the stars,
And the pismire is equally perfect,
and a grain of sand, and the egg of the wren,
And the tree-toad is a chef-d'oeuvre
for the highest,
And the running blackberry would adorn
the parlors of heaven . . .

—WALT WHITMAN

PICTURE PERFECT
Alice E. Heim

. . .

DAL AND I CELEBRATED OUR FIFTIETH WED-
ding anniversary in the fall of 1997 by taking a cruise in the
western Caribbean. Though Dal had been on many cruises,
courtesy of Uncle Sam's navy during World War II, this was
his first luxury trip and our first cruise together.

When the steward showed us to our cabin, the first thing
that caught my eye was a huge bouquet of red roses. Each
flower was perfect, so I took pictures of them because I was
sure they would soon fade. But something interesting happened: The flowers didn't fade. As if somehow imitating the
years that Dal and I have shared, those flowers remained fresh,
vibrant, and beautiful during our entire seven-day excursion.

When the cruise was over and it was time to disembark, those flowers looked the same as they had the day Dal gave them to me. And even though I had to leave them on the ship (you aren't allowed to carry flowers ashore), I felt as if those flowers and I shared something magical and symbolic. The flowers were more than just a symbol of my husband's love. They symbolized all of the lasting beauty that he and I have shared in the fifty years we've been together, and all of the lasting beauty that is yet to come.

DURING THE MIDDLE AGES, FINELY GROUND lily bulbs were often mixed with honey and used to heal burns and infections, treat snakebites, fight wrinkles, and restore bald spots.

The King James Bible contains at least fourteen citations about lilies, although the flower referred to as the lily might actually not be what we know as the lily today. *Lilium candidum* and *L. chalcedonium* are native to the Middle East and could be the lilies referred to in the Bible. The rose of Sharon in the Song of Solomon 2:1 is thought to be one of those species.

THE ROSE IS ONE OF THE OLDEST FLOWERS IN existence. Apple blossoms and peach blossoms are part of the rose family. The ancient Greeks and Romans were so fond of roses that they constructed warm houses to grow them out of season. Roses were used as garlands to decorate the large palaces, and petals were strewn on the floors. Wine known as rosewater was made from petals, and petals were dipped in sugar and used to decorate pastries. Dried rose petals were used to fill mattresses, which is where we get the expression "sleeping on a bed of roses."

Cupid used the rose as a symbol of love. In the Middle Ages, shrines were decorated with candles and garlands of roses. Respected in the Catholic Church, the rose was used for ceremonial purposes. The original rosaries were made of rosebuds and dried rose petals formed into a string of beads that were extremely fragrant. Fossil remains of roses are available for viewing in museums.

Tradition has it that a rose suspended from a ceiling provided approval for secrets to be discussed. Later, the rose was carved in wood and used in ceiling patterns to provide the space for secrets to be discussed "under the rose." Some landlords asked for unique roses to be used as payment for rents owed.

Rose oil is very valuable and is used as the base of many perfumes. Ointments for various purposes were made of rose oil and potpourri.

There is a time to plant and a time
to pluck up that which is planted.

—ECCLESIASTES 3:1–2

THE LEGACY OF THE
WEDDING CORSAGE
Alan Parkhurst

. . .

HAVING BEEN IN THE FLORAL INDUSTRY FOR many years, I have helped numerous customers plan elaborate weddings. Flowers are always a large part of this special day, and hours of care go into the details. Not so many years ago, this was not the situation. I have a treasured photo of my parents' wedding that makes me think of a different time. They were married during World War II, and like so many others, their lives were dramatically changed by the war.

The picture shows a beaming couple dressed not in traditional wedding garb but rather in very nice street clothes. My mom is wearing a wide-brimmed hat, and on her shoulder is a yellow rose corsage. That was the extent of their wedding's floral decor. It seems that they had planned a more elaborate elopement, but when the time came my father called with some distressing news: Someone had broken into his government-issued trunk and stolen their wedding money. He told my mother not to come to his air force base in South Carolina, but she went anyhow!

Because I made my living in the floral industry, I would often tease my mother about the corsage's being the only floral decor at her wedding. I would later include yellow roses as anniversary gifts to both of my parents when September 26 rolled around every year.

After fifty-six years of marriage, my precious mother died. While my father and I were going through her things after her funeral, we found his old government-issued trunk in the attic. Digging inside the trunk, we found the love letters they had sent to each other during their courtship. In a small box under the letters we found a very brittle, dried yellow rose corsage with a skeleton of plumosa foliage and a faded satin bow. It was a poignant discovery. The simple corsage that I had so often teased my mother about had been lovingly saved all those years.

Today I am the keeper of the yellow rose corsage. No, it isn't a valuable thing, not monetarily. But it is one of my prized possessions. Having relocated the fifty-six-year-old flower, I carefully tucked it away with all of the love letters and the photograph of the beaming couple on their wedding day. And each September 26, I am reminded of the love they had for each other and moved by the simplicity of the lasting wedding rose.

THE PEONY (*PAEONIA SUFFRUTICOSA*) IS HIGHly regarded in China and is understood to be the queen of flowers, signifying love, prosperity, and reverence. Chinese legend explains that a young student who grew numerous flowers, including the peony, was once visited by a young maiden who was quite taken by his garden. She was hired into the house as a servant and soon became a companion and lover to the student. One day, when he was expecting her, she did not arrive. He searched and searched until he finally found just a spiritual image of her fading into the wall of the home.

She told him that she was the soul of the peony in his garden and had been transformed into human form through his kindness and nurturing of the flowers. She could no longer stay because a moralist who was visiting the house didn't approve of the union, so she must return to the flowers. The student was devastated by the news and tried throughout the rest of his life to nurture a revisit from the stunning creature by tending his garden. She never reappeared, and the youth grew old in anticipation.

Marry when June roses blow
Over land and seas you'll go.

—WEDDING SUPERSTITION

PETALS OF RESPECT
Paula Westbrook

...

I WAS SAVING MYSELF FOR MY FUTURE HUS-
band. There were certain things I needed from a man before I
could physically give myself to him: I needed love and I needed respect.

I was a junior in college when Malcolm began pressuring
me for a more physical relationship. We had been dating for
only five months, and although I was somewhat flattered by
his attraction to me, I didn't feel I was getting what I needed
from him. We had a long talk one evening while we were out,
and I tried to make him understand my belief that there are
some things that are more important, more fulfilling, and
more enjoyable than sex. Initially, to my chagrin, Malcolm
couldn't fathom anything more enjoyable.

"I want respect, and right now I don't feel I'm getting any
from you," I explained.

Feeling frustrated and angry that I was being forced to
explain myself, I asked him to please just take me home.

Sulking with my girlfriends later that night in my dorm, I

couldn't help thinking about Malcolm and what had transpired between us. The rest of the night seemed endless, and the next day seemed to drag on forever. I had a feeling that I would never hear from Malcolm again. But I was mistaken. Late that afternoon I received a token of his respect and love in the shape of three long-stemmed roses and a card that read: "Just sharing my respects . . . you're welcome. Malcolm."

A year later we were married. Today, I still have that card—and I still have Malcolm.

THERE ARE OVER ONE HUNDRED SPECIES OF tulips, and although we used to be able to enjoy them only when they welcomed in the spring season, we are now able to enjoy them nearly year-round, since they are being grown in Europe and shipped around the world.

In the language of flowers, the red tulip is believed to represent a declaration of love; the yellow tulip speaks of a declared hopeless love. The variegated or streaked tulip says, "You have beautiful eyes."

A garden is a place to feel
the beauty of solitude.

—BOB BARNES

CORRESPONDING WITH TULIPS
Lynne Moss

. . .

SO OFTEN FLOWERS TAKE ON A SYMBOLIC ROLE in our lives. Take, for example, my story about tulips.

I had been corresponding with a very close friend for a long time over many miles and a stretch of ocean. It all began when he took a liking to me and sent me a card that read, "I know your love of flowers and yet I cannot spell CHRYSAN . . . mmmmm, so here's to TULIPS!!!"

From that day on, I became "Tulip" to him. Not only did I receive real tulips on special occasions, but I also received metal hand-crafted yard art tulips, built miles away and delivered to my doorstep. These are my "tulips to withstand time." The attached card read, "From a big bunch of tulips to a bunch of big tulips!!" In many ways, however, these age-old flowers, which traditionally stand for true love, were a constant tugging at my heart. Tulips kept us united, but never reunited us. They kept their independent, free spirit constantly tugging between us. No fairy-tale ending here, just a constant flow of energy and love between two people and a flower, transcending time and space.

We still keep in touch, though miles apart. I am forever "Tulip" to him. Tulips have become a symbol for the two of us, symbolizing the beauty and the strength of our relationship. And though we have never been reunited, there is a special unity between us that has everything to do with tulips.

ADDING THE BEAUTY OF FLOWERS IN THE MID-dle of winter is as easy as forcing bulbs into bloom on a window ledge. Their fragrance and visual excitement will add spirit and energy to a room. Tulips, narcissus, hyacinths, and crocus all work well.

You will need a cool room, cellar, or garage with a constant temperature between 45 and 50 degrees Fahrenheit. The refrigerator is a great place to get this process started.

Plant three to six bulbs in a six-inch clay pot using equal parts of potting soil, sharp sand, peat moss, and a little bit of composted cow manure, if available. Carefully place the bulbs on the soil. Fill around each bulb, leaving only a tiny piece of the bulb showing.

Soak the pots in a bucket of water or a filled sink until the soil mixture is thoroughly wet. To keep the soil in the pot, cover the pot with your hand when immersing it in the water. Then allow the pots to drain. The soil should be wet, but not drippingly wet!

Set the pots in a box and cover them with newspaper or cardboard to prevent the light from reaching the bulbs. Place the box in a space with a constant cool temperature.

In eight to twelve weeks the bulbs will begin to develop their own root systems, which will begin peeping through the drainage holes of the pot. Once the roots are formed and the new floral shoots begin to turn green and are four to six inches tall, move the pot to a sunny window. Always keep the soil moist.

These are the things I prize
And hold of dearest worth:
Light of the sapphire skies,
Peace of the silent hills,
Shelter of the forest, comfort of the grass,
Music of birds, murmur of little rills,
Shadows of clouds that swiftly pass,
And, after showers,
The smell of flowers
And of the good brown earth—
And best of all, along the way friendship and mirth.

—HENRY VAN DYKE

FIFTY YEARS
Russ Barley

...

WHEN MY PARENTS' FIFTIETH WEDDING anniversary rolled around, I knew that my siblings and I had to do something special. Our parents had given us so many precious and loving memories that we decided to give them a big celebration. Our parents didn't like the idea at first, saying they didn't really want us to do anything too extravagant. But it isn't often that children are able to celebrate such a special occasion with their parents, so we went ahead with our plans. We kept most of our intentions quiet, telling our folks only what they needed to know. I took my mother shopping for a new suit and helped my dad pick out his attire; my brothers and sister secretly ordered and sent the invitations, planned the food, designed the cake, hired a band, and chose decorations. I made a corsage for my mother and a boutonniere for my dad, using stephanotis blossoms from the plant I'd given my mother for Mother's Day several years before

When the special day arrived, tears came to my parents' eyes as we pulled up to their home in a limo. We had the driver take us to the Santa Rosa Beach Country Club, where we had cocktails and hors d'oeuvres while things were being secretly set up at my house for the best part of the celebration. After about an hour, we hopped back into the limo and headed for my house, where two hundred of their closest friends and family members were waiting for them. The tears in my mother's eyes and the look of surprise and joy on my father's face as we pulled in made it all worthwhile. The backyard was enclosed with a beautiful ivory tent, and all of the poles and edges of the tent were garnished with yellow-and-white flowers—lilies, roses, gerberas, and snapdragons. Tiny white Italian lights were used to add atmosphere. As decoration for the tent and the guest tables, I used over five hundred yellow roses symbolizing their fiftieth golden anniversary. Even the five-tiered wedding cake had yellow roses cascading down the sides. The flowers added so much flavor and zest to the party that friends still talk about them. It was a dream reception for everyone.

Later in the evening, while my mother and I were dancing to one of her favorite songs, she told me how appreciative she and my father were that we hadn't listened when they said they didn't want a big party. With tears in her eyes, she said how beautiful the flowers were and how wonderful the celebration was.

My mother is no longer with us; she died a little over two years after that party. It gives me great peace of mind that I was able to tell her how much I love her and to share all of those beautiful flowers with her. I will always remember her great passion for flowers, and I will never forget that flowers can say so much when the right words can't be found.

CANDLES GREATLY ENHANCE ROMANTIC EN-counters. The Romans developed candles containing wicks. The earliest candles were made of tallow, which gave off a strong odor and smoked profusely. Beeswax candles helped with these problems but did not appear until the Middle Ages. Today we use candles for the romantic mood they set, not for providing light in darkened houses.

Candles can be purchased that contain true essential oils that soothe mind, body, and spirit while enhancing a romantic affair.

Gently steed our spirits,
carrying with them dreams of flowers.

—WILLIAM WORDSWORTH

HEALING ROSE
Linda Wyszynski

...

OUR VACATION PLANS WERE ALREADY MADE when I went to the doctor for my yearly exam. My husband, Dennis, and I were driving to California in two days to see our niece, who is like a daughter to us. But during this routine exam the doctor made a discovery that posed a threat both to our plans and to my well-being. He found a lump in my breast.

Remaining calm, I asked if we could schedule a mammogram for after our trip, to which she replied that it shouldn't wait. She scheduled several tests for the very next morning. Leaving her office, I felt a little down and quite nervous. I called Dennis to tell him what the doctor had found and that we might have to alter our plans depending on the outcome of the tests. He was, as always, very optimistic, and tried to cheer me up. That evening he brought me a long-stemmed red rose. I was deeply touched. He held me and told me that we would get through whatever happened together.

I went in for my tests the next morning and, to my relief, was told the lump was only a cyst!

We decided to continue with our plans for vacation. The morning Dennis and I were leaving, I looked longingly at the rose and thought of the joy it had given me. This rose meant too much to leave behind. My husband's love, devotion, and willingness to stand beside me were manifested in the flower's perfect red petals. I returned the rose to the small water vial it had arrived in and decided to take it along. I found a "home" for it in our van, and we enjoyed it for several days as we drove through the western states on our way to California.

On the day I had to throw the rose away, Dennis said, "This rose meant a lot to you, didn't it?" I thought about how he has always found ways to demonstrate his love, like bringing me flowers to show that he's thinking about me. But I was especially touched by this rose. "Yes," I answered. "It showed me the love you have for me during the bad times as well as the good." And he responded with a long, loving look that warmed my heart and a smile that never fails to make my day.

FRAGRANCE IS FUNDAMENTAL TO OUR EXPERI-ence of flowers and gardens. A person will react instinctively to a beautiful bloom by putting it to his or her nose.

We carry scents in our minds, and they are

possessions that can carry us back to any time, any place.

All sorts of annual and perennial flowers, trees, shrubs, and vines add fragrance to a garden that changes through the seasons. When planting a garden, try to create a succession of scents rather than a riotous confrontation among the many fragrant possibilities.

Many flowers, such as lilies, are more fragrant in the evening. Emphasize the importance of plants that bloom after the end of the workday. The glowing and fragrant white flowers of the moonvine open at dusk. Night-blooming tropical water lilies are excellent exotic blooms. If you don't have a water garden, they can be grown in a tub on your deck. The peacock orchid (*Acidenthera bicolor*) is easy to grow and blooms profusely in late summer, releasing its fragrance at the end of the day. Lemon-scented daylilies, yuccas, angel's trumpet (*Brugmansia*), and four o'clocks can be included in a garden of night-blooming fragrant plants.

*My beloved is gone down into his garden, to
the beds of spices, to feed in the gardens and
to gather lilies. I am my beloved's, and my
beloved is mine: he feedeth among the lilies.*

—Song of Solomon 6:2–3

A Garden of Roses
JoAnn C. Schleis

. . .

World War II was a time of sacrifice. You
had to make do with what you had. The necessities always
came first, and no one complained. My parents married while
my father was in the army. During the time my father was
away fighting for our country, Mom was at home working
and saving. After the war, they began their life together with
what little she had saved. But the money in their bank account
wasn't important. To my parents, the importance of giving to
community and family was what mattered most. And that's
what they willingly did.

But as soon as they could scrape together a little extra
money, they built a grape arbor in our backyard and put up a
swing for my brother and me. They also planted florabunda
roses near a fence by the entrance to the backyard specifically because my mother loved them so.

Oh, those roses were gorgeous! Mother took such pride

in them, and everyone in our small, tightly knit community admired them. The clusters of flowers looked like bouquets hanging from the vines, and they seemed to bloom forever during the long summer months.

Years later, Dad accepted a position with a church-affiliated college, so we moved to another state. We settled in a big house in June, and Dad made sure that Mom had the plants for a new rose garden. They planted the roses together by the entrance driveway.

We moved twice more to other parts of the country. And we always had roses. Each home provided another plot to be nurtured with my parents' mutual love of roses. Together they found the best practices for growing the most beautiful roses. When they went fishing, they would catch fish specifically so my dad could bury them around the roses as fertilizer.

My mother wasn't selfish with those roses, either. She willingly shared them with anyone who would ask. I specifically remember one young man who asked if he and his bride-to-be could have some roses for their upcoming wedding. Of course, Mom was proud to share them, and I remember Dad's being even prouder that he had provided her with the roses to share. The roses provided both of them the means to share beauty, joy, and love with many people in their community. If someone became ill, Mom brought roses to cheer that person. She brought baskets of roses to decorate for special community-wide events, and cut individual roses to celebrate a personal relationship with a special friend. I remember that there was always one single rose in a vase on the kitchen table. I knew it was a sign of their love for each other.

After Dad retired they bought a travel trailer and spent a couple of winters at the Baja peninsula in Mexico before Dad found out he had cancer. The illness progressed quickly, and Dad was in and out of the hospital several times. They realized they wanted to be closer to family and made plans to move back to Colorado. Dad spent only four days in their new home before he was hospitalized for the last time. He passed away in November. In the spring, Mother planted roses. And I saw their love bloom all over again.

LEAVES CAN BE HARVESTED FROM INDOOR plants to use in floral arrangements. For best results, cut the leaves several hours in advance and place them in lukewarm water with floral preservative (packets of floral preservative are available from any floral shop). The leaves should be cut so that their stems are as long as possible without damaging the main plant.

Allow the leaves to sit in the water at room temperature for a few hours before arranging. Be sure the stem end is inserted into the water-soaked fresh floral foam when using so that the leaf maintains a source for nourishment.

If the leaves become spotted from water droplets, a light coating of spray leaf gloss should remove the stains. Be sure not to hold the can of spray too close to the leaves to avoid leaf burn. Lightly spray the underside of the leaf with an aerosol leaf shine, which will reduce the transpiration, or moisture evaporation, to increase longevity.

Flower in the crannied wall,
I pluck you out of the crannies,
I hold you here, root and all, in my hand,
Little flower—but if I could understand
What you are, root and all, and all in all,
I should know what God and man is.

—ALFRED, LORD TENNYSON

THE PRESENCE OF ROSES
Liz Bernstein

. . .

IT HAD BEEN A DIFFICULT SUMMER FOR MY daughter. She had graduated from college in June and decided to move in with my parents to be closer to her fiancé and her new job. There were more than a few adjustments to be made by everyone. Grandma had recently undergone cancer surgery, which had made mortality a very real issue. Grandpa was lovingly trying to keep Grandma as comfortable as possible.

Being a nurse, my daughter dealt with illness and death every day at the hospital, and she found it difficult to come home to her grandmother's pain. But she loved her grandma and knew how much her upcoming marriage meant to her. She spent many hours with her grandmother, sharing the news of the day and the plans for the wedding. Sometimes they just spent time looking out the window at Grandpa's lovingly tended garden as Grandma and Grandpa reminisced about their life together and shared love stories never heard before. Their love had survived the Great Depression and World War II. It was a bittersweet time for everyone.

As autumn and the wedding grew closer, Grandma became weaker. She and Grandpa often recited "their poem," which began: "Love is wanting you near me." Grandma seemed to know that her time was short, and she drew her family close. She shared feelings that hadn't been shared before and told everyone how much she loved them. She apologized for stealing attention away from my daughter's wedding and explained that, no matter what happened to her, she wanted the wedding to be the joyous occasion it should be. She didn't want there to be any sadness or sorrow. She had lived a long, solid, happy life, and now it was her granddaughter's turn to do the same.

Sixteen days before the wedding, Grandma quietly slipped away. The family's profound sadness became, in a sense, a combined strength. Grandma didn't want anyone to feel sadness or loneliness, so the wedding preparations continued. The family included Grandpa in all of the fuss and flutter, knowing all the time that his heart was breaking. He did, however, buy a new blue suit to wear for the occasion, just as Grandma had insisted. He faced the day with some trepidation, but persevered as he knew his wife would want him to.

The wedding day finally arrived. It was a cool October morning, and my daughter, the bride-to-be, and her sisters decided to dress at Grandpa's house in the room that had been Grandma's. The first pictures were taken in the garden that

Grandma had watched from her window and Grandpa had carefully groomed.

During the ceremony, Grandpa wept along with the rest of the family, tears that were a combination of joy and sadness. Then he read in the wedding program that the separate vase of white garden roses on the altar was in memory of Grandma. Grandpa cried with happiness, realizing that Grandma had made it to the wedding after all. This small gesture by his granddaughter, the bride, was a gift that celebrated the love her grandparents had shared through the years. What a joy it was for him to watch his beautiful granddaughter at the altar with her smiling new husband and the memory of her grandmother. When the minister quoted from I Corinthians that "love bears all things, believes all things, hopes all things, endures all things," our family understood it to be true.

The vase of white garden roses went to the reception and was placed with care on the family's table. Those flowers radiated the entire evening, just as Grandma would have, and seemed to laugh along with Grandpa as he danced to "YMCA" with his children, grandchildren, nieces, and nephews. At the end of the night, the roses went home with Grandpa.

The next morning arrived with that especially brilliant blue sky that comes only in October—or seems to. It is the kind of sky that supplies the soul with the strength to face the winter that lies ahead. Under that magnificent sky, Grandpa and his family took Grandma's roses to the cemetery. Her sweet soul had been present at the wedding, and now, with thanks, her family laid her to rest once more.

chapter five

The Language
of Love

THE FLOWER IS A LEAF MAD WITH LOVE.

— Goethe

The Circle of the Flame
Terrilynn Quillen

. . .

FLOWERS, LIKE PEOPLE, MUST BE AMONG God's prized possessions; he designs so many in such a wide array of color and shape. God has been very gracious in allowing me to enjoy the splendors of His creation through petals and people. Just as He has sent special people to me with spoken words of encouragement, He has also used the language of flowers to communicate His love for me and to set me on the right path in my journey on Earth.

My languishing soul was revived on a bright June day when a hot, sweaty, and nearly breathless young man came bounding onto the same tour bus I was riding. He was carrying a single orange rose, which he grandly presented to me as a show of his affection (we had both finished school and were on the same campus package tour). On seeing that single blossom my heart spoke to my mind, telling me that this man would someday be my husband. I held on to those thoughts— and to that rose—for months.

As the crisp orange rose dried and took on a mature kind of beauty, so had the relationship it foretold. Bill and I had been together for several months and had become very comfortable with each other, comfortable to the point where our relationship became predictable and even boring. I had grown accustomed to emotional roller coasters, with extreme highs and lows that kept me guessing. Bill never kept me guessing. I knew he loved me and I knew he hated roller coasters. Our relationship was more like a ferris wheel: no sudden turns, gasping drops, or surprises. Just predictably circular. I didn't know if I had what it took to make this relationship last. I'd been hurt so much in the past that I began to doubt myself and my ability to give Bill what he needed. I was afraid of losing him. I needed to know that he was going to stay. I needed to be sure. I longed for another grand display of unreserved devotion. Yes, the cute cards and daily phone calls kept coming, but I'd been through this routine before. The excitement dies, and pretty soon the man of your dreams is dreaming about someone else and you find yourself alone, with just a dumb old dried-up, should-be reminder of something as dead as the corsage you cry over.

I wasn't sure I could bear that kind of pain again, but somewhere within me I knew this relationship was worth preserving. I was reminded of the day of the tour bus, of my thoughts about Bill that day, and I turned to God in prayer, asking Him once again for flowers.

Christmas was coming, and I was feeling confident that my prayer would be answered. I was anticipating something really big and so foolishly romantic that the single orange rose would pale in comparison. I was looking forward to something like a dozen long-stemmed red American beauties, delicately wrapped in pearl-frost tissue in a satin-lined box, hand-tied with an exquisite black velvet ribbon, complete with a matching tiny black-velvet ring box tucked between the tissues. That would certainly do it.

"Well, what do you want for Christmas?" Bill asked.

"Just you, dear," I answered. But he insisted that he had to get me something. "Flowers will be just fine," I said. "I'm sure whatever you pick will be just perfect."

My heart leaped a few days later when I heard the doorbell ring and glimpsed a florist's van pulling from our driveway. I rushed down the stairs and flung open the front door, ready to whisk that long, slender boxed array of roses into my arms. Instead, I nearly stumbled over a bulky square brown cardboard box.

Opening the box, I found a rather mundane, yet elegant, table arrangement swathed in green waxed paper and fastened with ugly staples. Surely this couldn't be for me, I thought to myself. It was something you'd give to your mother, or your sister, or some other old lady. I looked at the envelope. Sure enough, it had my name on it. The card, edged in watercolor holly and ivy, bearing an Old English typeface declaring "Merry Christmas" was signed simply, "With All My Love, Bill."

As I peeled away the paper, I felt the bitter sting of disappointment. Yet, as I unmasked the arrangement, I became filled with awe and wonder over its beauty and simplicity—it consisted of a brass bowl full of mingled pine and other greenery, with a circle of poinsettias around a single red tapered candle. As I pondered the elements, I knew that God was speaking through Bill's gift. And I knew He loved me enough to send not what I wanted but what I needed, in His way, not mine.

I wondered if Bill realized that by sending a circle of poinsettias, evergreens, and a candle he was saying that our love was forever.

"What ever made you want to send me a Christmas arrangement?" I asked him later.

"Well," he said, "I thought everybody there in the house could enjoy it, not just you."

When I hung up the phone, I knew. Here I had found it. Not romance, but love. Love that is patient, love that is kind, never boastful, and most of all never selfish. Real love, the truest kind of all, the kind that comes perhaps only once, comes only with the help of God, and speaks in the language of flowers.

I know a bank where the wild thyme blows,
Where oxlips and the nodding violet grows
Quite over-canopied with luscious woodbine,
With sweet musk roses, and with eglantine.

—WILLIAM SHAKESPEARE

LOVE, SPEAKS THE HEART
Donna Herrin

...

MY HUSBAND, WAYNE, IS NOT A MAN WHO CAN easily express his feelings with words. He has other ways of showing his love for me, through considerate actions such as making me breakfast in bed or by jumping in to do household chores I normally take care of like doing the dishes. I have come to accept and love this man and his wordless demonstrations of love. His quiet ways never concerned me until we found out that he had leukemia. I worried that he would withdraw from me, keeping everything inside himself. I wondered what I could say or do to comfort and support him. I felt helpless.

It was difficult to know what Wayne was feeling about his illness; he never talked about it. I worried about him, but I was proud to see him go ahead with his plans to attend college in the fall to pursue his bachelor's degree. He was so sick, yet so determined.

One night he came home from class and handed me a hot cup of mocha and the prettiest mauve, cream-tipped rose I'd ever seen. I smiled, and he said, "Thanks for being so wonderful." My heart just squeezed with love for this dear man. I understood that the rose was his way of saying everything his heart was feeling. I knew that the rose was his way of thanking me for being there for him.

Wayne had a bone marrow transplant and is now cured of leukemia. I still have that cherished rose. When I look at it, I am reminded of that precious night when the words that were too difficult to say were spoken through the beauty of a rose.

SNAPDRAGONS ARE KNOWN AS GARDEN FLOWERS. But they're not just common garden flowers; snapdragons are fascinating, mysterious, and fun for adults and children alike. The snapdragon got its name because the individual florets look like a dragon's mouth. Gently squeezing the sides of each floret opens and closes the "mouth" of this dragon, and each floret can become a puppet for hours of summer playtime in the garden.

Although they can be grown easily in the garden all summer long, snapdragons are becoming increasingly available in retail establishments year-round. They can be purchased in many, many colors and are starting to be used for home decorating arrangements, as well as wedding designs.

The snapdragon is a tall, linear flower that responds to gravity. If laid on its side or placed at an angle in a container for any length of time, the head of the flower curves upward. Permanently curved stems can be created by laying a stem down for only one hour. To maintain snapdragons before arranging, always store upright, standing in a bucket or tub.

They last five to eight days and drink lots of water. Check the water level frequently and refresh. The lower florets can be removed as they begin to wilt, so the entire stem continues to mature and look fresh.

Happy are those who see beauty in modest spots where others see nothing. Everything is beautiful; the whole secret lies in knowing how to interpret it.

—CAMILLE PISSARRO

UNEXPECTED
Andrew Pike

...

SHE WAS A YOUNG GIRL IN HER FIRST YEAR OF college: wide-eyed, fresh-faced, and eager to experience the college life she'd heard so much about. She got involved in everything from sports to student government to the social life—as well as academics. And she thrived in this new realm of constant discovery.

When she met him for the first time, she was smitten. He did all the right things, said all the right words, and cared about her deeply. They were carried away by the emotions that surged through them, and things progressed rapidly. Too rapidly.

It was a beautiful afternoon when he got the call. She had been feeling tired, nauseous, and unusual, so she went to the clinic. She called him right away when the test results came back. She was pregnant. Although surprised, he wept when he thought about what she was experiencing, what they would be experiencing together. He went to see her, to hold her, and to discuss choices they never dreamed they would be forced to consider.

After hours of tears and talk, he returned to his room and she to hers. Each thought about how quickly their lives had changed. And each wondered what those changes meant for the future. He spent most of the night in prayer, asking God for strength, forgiveness, and above all, wisdom. He prayed that he would be able to care for and comfort her.

She trudged through her classes the next day, her concentration muddled with thoughts of the previous night. Listlessly, she wandered back to her dorm to think and to rest. But when she got there she found a surprise, something so unexpected that it brought tears of joy to her weary eyes. There before her was a magnificent bouquet of flowers. As she stepped closer to admire them, the beauty and the symbolism of the arrangement became clear. In the center of the bouquet, amid the gentle daisies and the rich carnations, proudly stood a single rose. Overcome with emotion, she opened the attached card that simply said, "I Love You."

FLOWERS WILL LAST LONGER WHEN PROPERLY conditioned and cared for. The steps for conditioning flowers include:

1. Don't ever use scissors to cut flower stems unless they are specially designed floral shears that won't pinch the stem and crush the stem cells, inhibiting water intake.

2. Always use a sharp knife for cutting and cut the stem at an angle. An angled cut exposes a greater area of stem for water intake.

3. Immerse the cut stem into water immediately, or better yet, cut the stem under water. A cut stem begins to scale over quickly, which reduces the number of cells open for water.

4. Prior to inserting the flowers into wet floral foam, allow the stems to absorb water for several hours.

5. Remove all foliage that is damaged and any excess foliage. All foliage that will be below the waterline should be removed automatically.

6. When cutting flowers from the garden, immediately immerse them in a bucket of water after cutting. When you bring them indoors to arrange, cut the stems again before you make your arrangement.

7. Flowers should be cut from the garden very early, or very late, in the day.

8. Change the water every few days to increase flower longevity. Stems shouldn't sit in fouled, decayed water.

*I am about to proclaim my audacity by assert-
ing the significance we must accord to grass,
silent, humble, the most obscure.*

—PLINY THE ELDER

RARE BEAUTY
Lillian Sibila

. . .

ODD AS IT MAY SOUND, WILDFLOWERS AND
weeds remind me of my late husband. Early in our marriage,
we were building a new home and raising two small children.
Money was tight, but we managed. We made do with what we
had and filled our home with the joy of love. We tried to keep
our expenses at a minimum, buying only the necessities.
Frivolous spending was not a luxury we enjoyed, which meant
that buying each other anniversary gifts was very difficult.

On one of our early anniversaries, I was sitting on the
front stoop of our home enjoying the early May sunshine
when my husband came around the corner carrying a bouquet
of wildflowers and weeds he had picked from the nearby
woods. He handed them to me shyly and sweetly.

"Happy anniversary, honey," he said, smiling broadly, his
face dotted with dirt and sweat.

Although we enjoyed many years together and would have

celebrated our fiftieth wedding anniversary in May 1996, I'll always remember that early anniversary more than the others. Gifts of the heart carry a certain rare beauty and charm that purchased gifts can't. That wildflower-and-weed bouquet meant more to me than all the gold and diamonds in the world. And watching my husband's face light up as he handed me his homemade gift is one of those memories that lasts forever.

WILDFLOWERS CAN BE USED TO ATTRACT BUT-terflies to your garden. Nectar-rich flowers provide good food sources for butterflies. Butterflies also love color. Their favorites are yellow, purple, blue, pink, and sometimes red flowers. Their favorite flowers include asters, Barbara's buttons, bee balm, butterfly weed, California fuchsia, cardinal flowers, wild columbine, coyote mint, fire pink, gay-feather, Joe-Pye weed, mountain mint, partridge pea, passionflower, phlox, and pine lily.

Fragrant wildflowers also draw a great deal of attention. These include Barbara's buttons, curly clematis, meadowsweet, Carolina phlox, Drummonds phlox, moss phlox, prairie phlox, summer phlox, spider lily, fragrant water lily, and sweet flag.

Essential oils are wrung:
The attar from the rose
Is not expressed by suns alone,
It is the gift of screws.
The general rose decays;
But this, in lady's drawer,
Makes summer when the lady lies
In ceaseless rosemary.

—EMILY DICKINSON

ROSES MEAN . . .
Kathleen Bretherick

. . .

BEING A FLORIST, I HAVE LEARNED THAT flowers speak many languages and say many things: flowers are used to express happiness and sadness; celebration and grief; new love, lasting love, and dying love. Sometimes the displays I create fill me with sorrow; at other times they fill me with joy.

Years ago, I received an order from a gentleman for twelve red roses to be gift-wrapped and delivered to a woman. This kind of order has always been a delight for me, thinking about the story behind the gift, trying to guess the occasion. Shortly after the flowers were delivered, however, my delight became confusion. The woman called to tell us that she did not want the flowers and asked us to come and take them away. Always trying to be helpful, our driver retrieved the flowers while I called the gentleman who had placed the order to explain the situation. The woman had to get those flowers, he explained. He was adamant about it, asking us to please deliver the flowers again. We did. One more time, our driver took the flowers to the woman's house, this time leaving them on her doorstep. Pretty soon, the woman was at the counter. She was visibly upset and flatly refused the roses. I didn't want to call the gentleman back, but I had no other choice. He wanted us to try one last time, and if the woman wouldn't accept them, we should do with them whatever we liked.

This put us in a very uncomfortable position. It seemed as though no matter what we did we weren't able to satisfy either customer or recipient. My heart broke for both of them. But rather than trying to deliver them again, I had the flowers delivered to a local hospice, where they were put in the church. I spoke with the minister, telling him the heartbreaking story. He was very kind and listened as I tried to make sense of the day's events. He told me that the roses had a home in the church and that a prayer would be said for the couple.

I never found out what happened. I never heard from the couple again. But I've frequently found myself thinking about them, and about the sad roses whose beauty failed to brighten one woman's day.

But sometimes the romantic power of flowers succeeds brilliantly.

A few years ago, a couple became engaged and the young man ordered a bouquet of yellow roses with one red rose.

When this couple got married, her bouquet was the same: yellow roses with one red rose. This became a tradition for the couple; on anniversaries, birthdays, and special occasions, the man would order his special gift. When their baby was born, he sent his wife one red rose each day while she was in the hospital and a bouquet of yellow roses when she arrived home.

He never sent a card, and over time we understood that he didn't need to; the red rose was the card, his distinct signature.

The couple's silver wedding anniversary was celebrated with the gift of yellow roses and one red rose. The tradition goes on. To me, this is true love and romance, and it inspires in me a feeling of warmth and joy.

Yes, roses mean different things to different people. They can mean the beginning, the end, or the endurance of time, but always, always, they mean love.

HISTORICALLY, *HYPERICUM*, WITH A HANDFUL OF varieties referred to as Saint John's wort, was used to foretell marriages. In Saxony, young girls were careful to place some Saint-John's-wort over their beds each night. If the plant remained fresh throughout the night, the girl was to marry within a year.

Concerning flowers' dreams
I will query the butterflies
even though they can't speak.

—REIKAN

THE ROSEBUD
Lillian Zarzar

...

IT WAS GIVEN TO ME ON THE OPENING NIGHT of *Charley's Aunt,* a play that Roger and I were performing in together. I was cast as Donna Lucia d'Alvadorez.

I materialized from my dressing room in costume, a turn-of-the-century traveling suit complete with parasol and fan, in character, awaiting my cue. As Roger approached me, the loud bustle of opening night anticipation became background noise and all of the last-minute, fast-paced activity surrounding us became a slow-motion blur. He and I were, however briefly, suspended in time and stillness. Looking intently at me, he handed me a delicate rosebud. Breaking the silence with his resonant voice, he said, "For you." I looked at him and became instantly captivated by his soft eyes gazing into mine. Without coming out of character, I said, "How kind of you." He chuckled quietly and then commented, "Ever the professional, in character already when you've yet to set foot on the stage." My character puffed up with pride and said,

"Of course." And my heart, the one beneath the character, responded with a rapid dance of joy. Holding the charming gift in my fingertips, I noticed that its white, translucent petals tipped with a velvety crimson gave off a delightfully subtle fragrance that seemed to envelop us, creating a lasting bond.

The rosebud adorned my dressing room table throughout the three-week run of the play, its sweet smell evoking the memory of the moment it was given. Eventually, it dried and transformed into a uniform beige color. And although the translucence dulled and the light faded, it maintained a fragile beauty by never opening into a full bloom. I saved the dried flower, having become so attached to it, in a clear Lucite box with a rosebud carved on the lid.

The bond that Roger and I created remained intact for a few years, but over time things changed and we lost contact. We went on with our lives. He married and had two children; I became engaged but never married. He stayed in the same city while I traveled the world. But I never forgot him. As I moved around from place to place, I carried the rosebud with me as a constant reminder of that very special moment.

Two decades later, when my phone rang one day and I heard that familiar resonant voice, my heart responded again with joy. Roger had searched me out, wanting to call and catch up on what had been happening in our lives over the past twenty years.

After many phone calls and e-mails, we were reunited, and on our first date I showed him the rosebud that I had kept all those years. Roger recognized the lovely, faded rosebud that had never bloomed, tears forming in his eyes. He wasn't aware of the feelings that had prompted me to cherish the flower and was deeply touched that I'd kept it all those years. That flower represented a significant point in our lives, and now that we are reunited in a fresh new relationship, that rose reminds us that our relationship was born many years ago and, regardless of the years in between, has truly stood the test of time.

The rosebud now sits on my dressing table at home, still in its Lucite box. It took a while and a lot of long-distance correspondence, but the bloom finally came—in our hearts. Roger and I are performing together again, only this time on the stage of life.

THE GREEK GODDESS APHRODITE IS THE GOD-dess of love and beauty. Her counterpart in Roman mythology is Venus. It is said that Venus was the original source of the red rose. The story tells that she always carried a white rose, then one day she pricked her finger and began to bleed, staining the petals of the white rose for-ever. Sometimes the rose is featured in the crown of Venus or on the scepter she holds.

The legend of Cupid says that it was he who stained white rose petals red after he spilled wine on them.

The language of flowers suggests that roses

stand for love and beauty. In Victorian times, roses were the customary flower to weave into chaplets for the crowns of brides and brides-maids.

Prior to the 1500s not many roses grew in Europe. In the 1700s, long-stemmed varieties, including the intoxicatingly beautiful tea rose, arrived from China. Shortly after that, growers started hybridizing roses.

In the organic world, the more obscure
and feeble the reflection,
so much the more does grace extend,
radiating and sovereign.

—HEINRICH VON KLEIST

FREE LOVE IN THE GARDEN
Charles Goodwin

. . .

MY WIFE OF FORTY YEARS DIED FIVE YEARS
ago from cancer. Esther and I did everything together—from
working our farm, to raising our four children, to sitting on
the front porch of our farmhouse at the end of a long day, just
being together. When she died, I thought my life was over, too.

Keeping my small farm running became harder and harder.
The following fall, my children convinced me to sell it and move
into a town house near two of them. Although I missed my old
house, suburban life was not hard to get used to. I found friends
at a community senior center that was within walking distance,
and I took planned trips with others of my own age. Over time,
though, what I found I really missed was planting and growing
things. I tried a few pots on my porch, but it just wasn't the same.

I found out that our city had community garden plots that
were offered free to residents on a first-come first-served basis. The
next spring I signed up for one. The plot was twenty feet square
and was surrounded by chain link fence to keep out the animals.

I started planning my garden. Flowers would be along the

perimeter—Peace roses, gladioli, snapdragons, and purple iris (my favorite). Vegetables would be in the center—tomatoes, beans, squash, and corn. The work started. I buried myself in cultivating, planting, fertilizing, watering, and weeding. Little sprouts turned into healthy plants that started to have flowers or signs of fruit. Everything seemed to do well except my iris plants. Instead of having that sense of pride in growing things, I started to really miss my old farm. I missed Esther even more.

The nicely manicured plot next to mine was leased to a woman named Rose. She worked in her garden almost every day. She always wore a wide-brimmed straw hat and used floral printed gloves when she worked. At first, we would acknowledge each other only with a smile and a brief hello. Never overly friendly, but not rude either. We just respected each other's space.

One day Rose commented about my Peace roses, saying that they were her favorite flower and that she always had a hard time growing them. We talked for a while about roses in particular and gardens in general. I told her that I admired her purple iris plants and mentioned how I had tried to grow some earlier but they just did not take. After a few more minutes of chatting, I found out that she was recently widowed and lived a few miles away. We bid each other a good day and went back to work.

The next day, I took a cutting from one of my Peace rose plants and started the process of rooting the rose. I learned this process from my father many years earlier. Over the course of time, the cutting did root, and so did the relationship that was building between Rose and me. The following spring, I gave her the rooted rose for her garden. To my surprise, she had dug out some of her iris plants to give to me on the same day!

I know I will never forget my Esther, but with my children's encouragement and our love for flowers, Rose and I began slowly to fall in love. We became husband and wife early in 2000 and are both looking forward to this new chapter of love and romance in our lives. We still have our individual garden plots, but there is no longer a chain link fence separating them.

A SUNFLOWER PLAYHOUSE IS FUN TO GROW and is a great place for children—along with their parents and grandparents—to spend afternoons of fantasy. Plant six to eight giant sunflowers a few feet apart in a circle. After the sunflowers have grown about a foot high, plant morning glories or clematis around the base of each flower. These will climb up the sunflower stems and fill in the open spaces between them. When the sunflowers are about six feet high, place a web of string or twine across the space between the heads of the sunflowers, for the morning glories or clematis to grow along forming a roof and creating a protected circle beneath. Spanish moss can be placed on the roof and even tucked into the spaces between the stems to add texture, variety, and sun-blocking qualities to the structure of your playhouse.

Come forth into the light of things.
Let Nature be your teacher.

—WILLIAM WORDSWORTH

THE ODD COUPLE
Angela Ronemark

...

MY SECOND HUSBAND, BOB, AND I MET AT A local garden center. Wanting information about mulch, I neared the information counter just as I heard a handsome guy ask the clerk the same question that I was going to ask. After getting the answer we were looking for, Bob and I started talking about our respective gardens. During the course of our conversation, we realized that we were both single parents. Bob saw that I was getting quite a few bags of mulch, and he asked if there would be anyone home to help me unload them. Knowing where he was going with this question, I had to think quickly. If I said no, Bob would probably offer his assistance. If I said yes, I might never again see this guy who seemed pretty nice. So I took a chance and said that I would be spreading the mulch myself while my babysitter was watching my two sons. Well, just as I thought he would, Bob offered to come over and help unload the bags for me.

When we arrived at my house, the sun was already beating down and the midday heat was oppressive. Bob unloaded my fifteen bags of mulch and helped me spread it around my flowers and plants. With two of us working, it didn't take long to get the job done.

Later we enjoyed a glass of iced tea together on my deck as he shared how impressed he was with my neatly maintained, orderly garden. I had plants in neat rows, taller plants behind shorter ones, like colors together. As we talked, I found that I really enjoyed the company of this man who seemed to be free-spirited and fun. That weekend, we went out to dinner at a very nice restaurant. I was a bit nervous because it was the first "date" I had been on since my divorce ten months earlier. What an enjoyable evening we had, filled with fun conversation on many subjects. Naturally, we discussed gardening in depth and shared stories about our favorite flowers. Surprisingly, we found that we both used our gardens to share life lessons and instill values into our children. He couldn't wait to show me his garden, and I agreed to visit him with my two sons, Jason and Justin, on Sunday afternoon.

He and his children, Amanda and Mark, greeted us warmly when we arrived. Amanda and Mark excitedly told us all about their garden. Jason and Justin were much more controlled and not quite sure how to take these enthusiastic new friends. What a shock we had when we got our first look at their garden! Although the plants looked extremely healthy— full, lush, filled with blooms—the garden itself looked wild! No order, no reason, just stuff planted everywhere. I gulped silently and gave my sons a don't-say-anything motherly look when they turned to me, ready to make what would surely be a critical comment about the garden. Bob, Amanda, and Mark were very proud of their garden, though. They went from side to side, showing me everything, telling me where each plant came from and what it meant to them. I could tell that this family was passionate about their garden! They seemed so lovingly happy with each other and so excited to be together. All this excitement became contagious, and before the afternoon was over, I realized that Justin, Jason, and I were laughing more than I could ever remember us laughing at one time before. We found our new friends very refreshing and in some ways healing to our souls.

The day passed, and Bob and I dated for about a year, sometimes with all the children, and sometimes just Bob and I. We found that our separate habits of orderliness and chaos were evident in other parts of our lives and realized that a challenge existed—as did an opportunity. Together we learned that there is a place for order and a place for chaos and that the trick is to balance the two. We were married in 1997. Now our blended family works together in a garden blessed with both Bob's passion for abundance and my love of order.

GYPSOPHILA IS ANOTHER NAME FOR BABY'S BREATH, one of the most commonly used florals. *Gypsophila* adds a light, airy touch to floral designs and can soften moods and enhance themed arrangements. It is most often used to fill in around the larger and more colorful flowers in an arrangement.

Baby's breath is available in many varieties. Some of the newer varieties, such as Million Stars, have full clusters of tiny bright white flowers, sparse foliage, and flexible stems. These varieties look especially beautiful when placed in a vase on their own.

Simply gather several stems together in a generous bunch, trimming off excess flowers, adding and trimming until a soft mounded shape is formed. Cut the stems to the appropriate length for the container chosen. Remove any foliage that might be under water. Place in a container filled with cool water that has been enriched with a floral preservative.

Where would we be if humanity had never known flowers? If they didn't exist and had always been hidden from view . . . our character, our morals, our aptitude for beauty, for happiness: would they be the same?

—MAURICE MAETERLINCK

FLORAL RITUALS
Elaine Schmidt

. . .

MY PARENTS GREW FLOWERS, LOTS OF FLOWERS of all shapes, sizes, and colors. Some of my fondest memories involve helping them plant, weed, water, and fertilize the gardens that surrounded our home. When they retired they started a small dried flower business, giving demonstrations and selling finished floral designs. Flowers created a strong bond between me and my parents. It is no wonder that flowers are my favorite motif and I constantly look for ways to surround myself with reminders of these happy times.

When my husband and I married on October 21, 1972, a new ritual began in my life. One just as important as the rituals surrounding flowers throughout my childhood. Each month when the twenty-first rolls around, my husband, Kenny, brings me flowers. Sometimes the surprise is a simple mixed bunch from the local grocery store; at other times it might be a flat of annuals ready for planting outdoors in the springtime.

Even during the lean years that every couple experiences, this ritual did not falter. When he couldn't afford to purchase flowers, he would stop along the roadside and pick a bunch of Queen Anne's lace to surprise me.

Throughout the years I always knew I could count on this presentation of flowers each month, just as I grew to know that I could always count on my husband. This solid trust is what makes a marriage last. But ours hasn't just "lasted," it has blossomed and grown throughout the years through this ritual of flowers we both treasure.

Every time one of my friends marries, I share our story of flowers with them and encourage them to form a strong, lasting floral ritual in their new life together. I even help the process along by giving them a special wedding gift—a beautiful vase so they can begin their own tradition of love.

ROMANTICS OF ALL TYPES LOVE LILIES. Vibrant, colorful, aromatic, lilies have much to offer lovers. They do, however, present a unique problem. Their long, luxurious anthers, ablaze with color, are also full of pollen that gets more abundant as the flower matures. It drops from the flower and is notorious for staining tablecloths, rugs, clothing, and even skin. Use a tissue or gloved hands to simply pull off the anthers as the flowers open.

*If seeds in the black earth can turn
into such beautiful roses, what might not
the heart of man become in its
long journey toward the stars?*

—G. K. CHESTERTON

FLOWERING TOGETHER
Rosemarie Rossetti

. . .

I PLANTED MY OWN FLOWERS THIS YEAR. FOR most people that's no big deal. For me, it is. Eleven months ago, I became paralyzed from the waist down after a tree fell on me while I was bicycling. In the past I have taught horticulture at the Ohio State University, written a popular textbook on houseplants, and truly enjoyed every minute I could spend in the garden.

My motto since being paralyzed has been "Do something new every day." At my request, my physical therapist, Laura, helped me figure out how I could plant annuals at home in the front yard. She simulated the process on the carpeted floor in the therapy room, showing me how to balance myself on the palm of one hand, as well as on a clenched fist. There I was, out of my wheelchair and on my hands and knees for the first time. Planting flowers seemed possible again.

In the days that followed, I continued to practice at home. I would get out of my wheelchair onto the floor. Once on the floor, I managed to get myself up on my hands and knees and stretch out my thighs. Then came my first attempts to crawl forward on all fours. Baby steps. First a hand, followed by a knee. Progress was slow. I could crawl ten feet in my carpeted living room, from the couch to the stairs and back. I made up my mind that I was going ahead with my gardening plan.

I drove my husband, Mark, in my new hand-control-operated van to the local garden center. In my chair, I wheeled around the aisles, trying to envision what I wanted the garden to look like. Flats of deep pink petunias caught my eye, then flats of purple and pink dianthus drew my attention.

The sale was completed, and Mark loaded the flats into the van. Headed for home, I was ecstatic that I would once again be able to garden. Just eleven months before, as I lay in intensive care, once again doing simple everyday tasks, including gardening, seemed impossible. Now I was getting my life back. Granted, things were different, but I was able to function and resume some of my previous activities.

But although learning new ways to do old things on your own is important to anyone who has been paralyzed, the support of loved ones is also essential. Mark has been by my side every step of the way, allowing me my freedom but ready to step in and help in a subtle way when he sees that I need it. We've needed to become a life team in ways that most married couples never imagine. I am an independent person by nature. For most couples, independence is a given; for me, even independence relies on the support of others.

So, although I say "I" planted the flowers, it was really a team effort. After Mark unloaded the van, we decided to wait a day for planting. I surveyed the front flower beds once more to make sure that we had bought enough flowers. I felt confident that we had enough to go around.

The next morning, Mark positioned a flat of dianthus directly in front of the bed. I crawled out of the chair and knelt on a foam pad. Crouched on my knees with a hand trowel in position, I dug my first little hole. Then I took hold of one of the small packs of dianthus and popped out one of the tiny seedlings, lowered the plant into the hole, and filled in the area with soil and gently tamped the surface. I inched my way around the perimeter of the flower bed, and another plant was set.

As I reached the end of the line, I sat back to rest and admire my work. Neighbors drove by grinning as they saw me in my yard again. It was obvious by my broad smile and my fervent wave how much I loved gardening.

Many of the areas of the planting bed were hard for me to reach. Mark agreed to finish planting those areas. Soon he ran out of flowers and told me he would be back with more. A few hours later he returned with several more flats of white petunias and an assortment of other flowers that he'd found appealing. There seemed to be so many flowers! *Where is he going to put them?* I thought.

I suggested that he look out the windows of the second story of our house before he began in order to look for empty spaces. He concurred and quickly returned to plant the second batch of flowers.

Several hours later, he came in to shower. "Boy, those flowers sure look good, honey. You did a great job!"

Later that evening, I had a chance to admire our work. I could see that Mark had gone a little overboard, since the flowers were densely spaced. As the season progressed, the flowers created a garden of abundance never before seen in our yard. Mark carefully watered, fertilized, and weeded the beds. Ideal conditions produced the most gorgeous flower beds imaginable! We were drawing crowds in our neighborhood, just to take a peek. It was clear that Mark and I made a perfect gardening team. In the days that followed, not only did our love for gardening grow but so did our love of life and each other.

SUMMER ROMANTICS CAN USE SUNFLOWERS TO add excitement and interest to the environment of a relationship. During the late summer, gardens and fields are overflowing with sunflowers, named because the face of the flower always turns toward the sun. Large or miniature sunflowers can be used with simple glassware and white ceramic containers to add a fresh, just-picked look to a room setting.

You can express the feeling of a country home through weathered barn siding, straw, and wicker.

Place sunflowers in an oversized glass vase filled with water and whole lemons. Refresh the water often.

Use a raffia or twig wreath to tie back a curtain. Place a sunflower in a florist's tube and tuck into the tieback.

To dry sunflowers, simply hang them upside down or allow them to dry on the stem. Use dried sunflower heads to decorate a wreath. Hang on an outside door or wall and your little feathered friends will be able to dine all winter long on the seeds.

They shall still bring forth fruit in old age;
they shall be fat and flourishing.

—PSALMS 92:14

THE HUG TREE
Julie Woodell

. . .

MY HUSBAND, DAVE, AND I HAD BEEN MAR-
ried for only three months when his National Guard unit was
called up for Desert Storm duty. We lived in an apartment and
had a balcony that faced a field where we would play softball
and volleyball with the other tenants. I remember sitting on
that balcony with Dave in the days before he left, dreaming
about our future and the house we would buy when he
returned. It would have flower gardens, trees, and room
enough for our family to grow. But those plans would have to
wait. In the meantime, we tried to take advantage of every
minute we could together as his date of departure drew closer and closer.

The day before Dave was to leave, he went to visit his
parents. I was in the kitchen preparing his going-away dinner
when he returned. Hearing him go out to the balcony, I went
out to give him a hug and kiss. He was just placing the pot of
a miniature hibiscus tree on the balcony floor. The tree had
flower buds on the tips of several branches, and one of the
magnificent flowers was in full bloom. My heart was racing.

He turned toward me slowly. I looked deeply into his clear blue eyes and felt our souls connect. After a moment of silence, he told me that he had chosen this tree as a going-away present for me. He said that although he would be very far away in body, he would be only as far away as our balcony in spirit. Dave told me that each time a new hibiscus flower appeared, it was a hug from him. When I got lonely, I should think about all the hugs that he was sending my way.

Boy, was I a wreck! Just thinking about what he was going to be facing made me cry. But the beautiful tree gave me something to hold on to. It made me think of Dave as alive and fighting to be able to come home to me.

As the weeks went by, my normal routine included a morning trip to the balcony, where I would carefully check my hug tree. I felt connected with Dave in a way that words cannot describe. When there was a new bloom, I just sat down and looked at it, imagining in my mind his warm arms around me, saying that everything was all right.

Dave did return safely months later. Our hug tree is much larger now and is continually full of bright orange flowers. It looks beautiful on the large porch of our new house, and our two children often ask to hear the story of how the hug tree connected their mommy and daddy through time and space.

chapter six

Unexpected Surprises

THE FLOWERS WE MOST LOVE ARE THOSE WE
KNEW WHEN WE WERE VERY YOUNG, WHEN OUR
SENSES WERE MOST ACUTE . . . AND OUR
NATURES MOST LYRICAL.

—*Dorothy Thompson*

THE TWELFTH ROSE

Nori Gartner-Baca

...

For our first Valentine's Day together, we planned a nice trip to Toronto. It would also be our first weekend away together. The amount of time it took us to drive from Rochester, New York, to Toronto surprised both of us, and the car we were in didn't inspire confidence as we crossed the border. But we made it, even though the car was sputtering loudly as we pulled into the parking lot of our hotel. After checking in we realized how hungry we were. We hadn't planned well enough to have Valentine's Day dinner reservations, but luckily the hotel's restaurant looked cozy and available. And so we threw our things into our room and headed back downstairs for the restaurant.

Almost immediately after we were seated, I noticed him staring blankly at me. "Are you okay?" I asked.

"Uh, no. I have a terrible headache," he blurted out mechanically. "I'm going to the room to get some aspirin," he added, then left.

Nearly twenty minutes later the waitress filled my water glass for the third time. Still no sign of him. I could feel myself getting angry. Should I have gone with him? Should I go check on him? Should I stay there, alone in a strange restaurant in a strange city on Valentine's Day? Sick? Did he say he was sick? In all the time I had known him, he'd never been sick. I'd never known him to suffer from a stomachache or a cold, a hangover or a headache. My foot jerked with anger as I looked up and saw him coming back.

"Feel better?" I asked, attempting to mask my irritation. I was glad that he was back.

"Yes," he said. Long pause. "No."

"No, you don't feel better?" I asked, confused by his answers.

"Yes. No," he replied.

"Do you want to leave?" I asked, agitated. When I got no answer, I finally suggested that we go back to the room to lie down, hoping a good night's sleep would shake him out of his weird mood. He agreed, but when the elevator door opened on our floor, he darted out ahead of me. I ran to catch up just as he was shutting the room door on me.

"What are you doing?" I asked, exasperated.

"Nothing. Um, just wait a minute," he said.

After what felt like an eternity, the door opened a crack and I was invited in. The room was dark, but just as I reached for the light switch I noticed candles burning. As my eyes adjusted to the darkness and I scanned the room to find him, I saw the roses. Long-stemmed roses were everywhere. I picked up the one closest to me, smelled it, and smiled. All of my worries about his strange behavior disappeared.

"There are a dozen roses hidden throughout the room," he began, a small smile spreading across his face. "And when you find all of them," he added, "you'll get your present."

"Presents!" I cheered, and set off to find the hidden flowers. After finding all but one, I looked up at him and whispered, "One more."

"Just one more until your present," he said, smiling at me.

I kept looking, unable to find that one last rose. I looked in the same places, as though I'd somehow missed it.

"Honey, maybe they only gave us eleven flowers," I said, bending to smell the roses and to touch the soft petals—and to look for a second time under the bed, in the dresser drawers, and behind the curtains.

"No, there have to be twelve. I bought a dozen, and there'd better be twelve," he said defensively, as though it would be his fault if the bouquet were a rose short. He looked around the room and asked me to check behind the table. I assured him that I'd already looked there, but he said maybe I should check there again. "Okay," I said, shrugging. I wanted him to just give up on the last flower and enjoy the ones we had—and give me my present. I wasn't selfish, but making me wait this long for my surprise was agony. As I moved the chair to search again, he quickly closed in behind me.

"I found it!" he cheered, and as I turned I saw him pull it from behind his back.

"Very tricky," I said with a grin. As he handed me the last rose, I noticed that there was a pink ribbon tied around the stem.

"This is your present," he whispered, stepping closer.

I took the end of the thin pink ribbon in my fingers and asked, "What am I supposed to do? Wear this?"

"No," he said, sliding my hand down the ribbon. As our hands came together at the end of the pink strand, he lifted my chin and said, "You wear this." I followed his hand with my eyes, and there, tied gracefully at the end, was a diamond ring. I stared in disbelief, and before I knew it, he was down on one knee proposing. I began to tremble. I grabbed for his hand as tears streamed down my face.

"Yes, yes. Yes. Yes!" I replied, laughing and crying at the same time, hugging him tightly.

For the rest of the weekend we were sure that we must have looked different. After all, an engaged couple looks different, or so we thought. We floated through the remainder of the trip and barely stumbled back into reality when we got home.

Now, three years later, a wreath made from those twelve engagement roses hangs above our living room couch as a constant reminder of my husband's ability to fake a headache and make me the happiest woman in the world!

IN THE VICTORIAN LANGUAGE OF FLOWERS THE
violet came to mean faithfulness.

William Hunnis wrote a poem at the end of
the 1500s titled "In a Nosegay always sweet, for
lovers to send for tokens of love at New Year's
Tide, or for fairings." It reads:

> *Violet for faithfulness*
> *Which in me shall abide;*
> *Hoping likewise that from your heart*
> *You will not let it slide.*
> *And will continue in the same*
> *As you have now begun,*
> *And then for ever to abide,*
> *Then you my heart have won.*

Now he that planteth and he that watereth
are one; and every man shall receive his own
reward according to his own labor.

—1 CORINTHIANS 3:8

AN OFFICER AND A GENTLEMAN
Cheryl Runstrom

...

AS THE TRAIN SPED ALONG THE EAST COAST toward Florida, tears silently slid down my cheeks. The complications of modern family life can seem overwhelming, particularly when it comes to transporting children between parents and states. I was on an arduous thirty-six-hour train trip. I had just delivered my children to their father, my ex-husband, in New Jersey for a long visit and was returning to my home in Florida. As the train made its way along the many miles, I contemplated the lonely months I would now spend without my kids and the lonely evening that lay ahead. I thought my husband was out at sea and I was feeling sad that he wouldn't be there to comfort and reassure me when I arrived home.

It was almost 5:30 A.M. when the train, quiet with sleepy passengers, approached the station in Jacksonville. Suddenly I heard a buzz coming down through the long, dark train car; soft whispers filled with excitement and awe made their way to my ears. I looked out the window and up the tracks to see what had everyone in such a frenzy. As we reached the platform, I saw the profile of a handsome naval officer, suited up in formal dress whites and holding a huge bouquet of yellow roses. His hat was low over his eyes and he stood proud.

Oblivious to the crowd that had eagerly gathered to watch, I ran to that handsome naval officer, my husband, and threw myself into his arms. After a long kiss, I buried my nose in the yellow roses and knew that I was home—and that I was loved by a very special man.

THE ART OF MAKING POTPOURRI DATES BACK to long before the time of the pharaohs. Historically, it was used to mask odors from poor sanitation as well as to ward off insects. In French the word *potpourri* means "rotten pot." Today potpourri is simply a mixture of dried flowers and other ingredients used to add fragrance to a room.

I will make thee beds of roses
And a thousand fragrant posies.

—CHRISTOPHER MARLOWE

A ROSE BY ANY OTHER NAME . . .
IS STILL AN ALLERGY
Elaine Gartner

. . .

MY HUSBAND AND I HAD A CLASSIC WHIRL-
wind courtship complete with romantic dinners, music, surprises, and exciting times but with one glaring and romantic
exception—no flowers.

I never knew why I did not receive flowers, but because I
was in love, it didn't matter.

It was not until after we were married in 1965 that the situation was remedied. Shortly after our wedding, whenever
there was an occasion to celebrate—like birthdays, anniversaries, or Valentine's Day—my husband would delight me
with flowers, mostly roses, and a romantic card delivered
directly to our home.

I loved the sight and smell of these bouquets of love,
which, on our just-out-of-college-with-lots-of-debt budget,
were doubly meaningful. However, I also came to realize that
these beautiful creations almost always led me to tears. Not
tears of romantic emotion or joy but allergy tears, complete
with itching eyes, sneezing, and sniffles.

I refused to acknowledge the possibility of an allergy to

flowers and tried to hide the effect the roses had on me. Sensing that I might be allergic to them, one day my husband sent me a bouquet of mixed flowers with lots of ferns and other greenery but no roses. Unfortunately, after a couple of hours I once again began my allergic routine.

My husband felt terrible each time I received his lovely flowers and had to go straight to the medicine cabinet for antihistamines. So, for many, many months, he sent me no flowers. Sadly, he sent me nothing at all . . . nothing to fill the void with any other romantic item. I felt ignored and hurt and missed the sense of romance.

Realizing his omission, he eventually asked what kind of flower I thought might not cause an allergic reaction. I jokingly replied, "A cactus flower."

The next day, a beautiful flowering cactus arrived at our door. It was exquisite, with a tall stem and a beautiful flower—a fantastic tribute to my husband's love and ingenuity. More important, I had no allergic reaction. It was great. I could stare at one of God's beautiful and mystifying plants and be reminded of how much my husband truly loved me.

But, while trying to relocate my new treasure in our living room, I managed to scratch myself quite badly on the cactus plant. As luck would have it, my husband witnessed my struggle and came to my rescue after grabbing some work gloves. He relocated the cactus without injury to himself or the plant.

Throughout the next couple of years, my husband sent me a few cactus gardens and individual plants, including an aloe plant to help heal my wounds. Somehow, though, I almost always managed to hurt myself in some way as I cared for them.

Eventually, he concluded that I suffered from a different kind of allergy, which surfaced whenever a cactus plant and I came into contact—clumsiness. Thus, a change in plans was essential if he was going to maintain some romanticism in our marriage and not single-handedly support the bandage and peroxide manufacturers.

My husband's solution was unique and I will treasure it always.

One summer afternoon, he returned home from a trip to the local shopping center carrying a large package wrapped in kraft paper with a bow on top and a small, beautifully wrapped box. He told me that he could no longer watch me suffer with allergies to roses, flowers in general, and cactus plants, and presented me with my presents.

Before letting me open my gifts, he told me that, at first, I might not consider them to be romantic items. But he promised (and we never made promises we could not keep) that eventually I would come to appreciate the true nature of the gifts.

My curiosity piqued, I ripped open the paper to discover a plain, unstained pine bar stool. I was speechless! I stared incredulously at him, wondering in which extraterrestrial guidebook he had discovered that a bar stool might be a romantic gift. He just motioned me toward the other, smaller box, and I sarcastically asked if it contained a can of stain. "No," he said, the hurt in his voice. So I opened the second package, trying desperately to envision something, anything, romantic.

Inside was a bottle of my favorite after-dinner liqueur—Bailey's Irish Cream. Again, I was forced to just stare at him, trying to connect the two gifts and figure out how they could be considered the least bit romantic.

At that point, my wonderful husband picked up the stool and walked to our dining room window, which faced our neighbor's beautiful flower garden. Because of my allergies, I was unable to raise flowers myself, so I used to watch them bloom from afar.

He positioned the stool in front of the window, poured me a large snifter of Bailey's, and handed me the drink. Then he edged me toward the stool, asking me to sit down. He said, "Take time to smell the roses from the safety of our house, and love me always."

THE BASIC INGREDIENTS FOR POTPOURRI ARE fragrant flowers, leaves, herbs, and spices; colorful blossoms and leaves; fixatives to hold the fragrance; and essential oils.

The fragrant flowers that I like to include are roses, marigolds, jasmine, carnations, anemones, scented geraniums, and peonies. I use foliage such as eucalyptus and bay leaves for their distinct scents. The pungent fragrances of herbal chamomile, feverfew, lavender, lemon verbena, sage, rosemary, artemisia, thyme, basil, and mint are pleasant additions to

198 · Flowers Are for Love

a potpourri mixture, as are spicy cinnamon, star anise, clove, mace, and nutmeg.

I add a vibrant look with bachelor's buttons, zinnias, globe amaranth, salvia, delphiniums, pansies, and violets. Dried peels from lemons, limes, oranges, and grapefruit add interesting texture and color.

Fixatives include orrisroot powder, ground gum benzoin, and crumbled cinnamon sticks. Oil of sandalwood, clove, or patchouli can also be used. A general rule of thumb is to use a tablespoon of fixative for every cup of dried materials.

Essential oils are the pure oils of a flower, spice, or herb. All ingredients contribute to the blend, but the essential oil dominates the potpourri mixture. Only a few drops are used at a time. More can be added as the fragrance dissipates.

When making potpourri, all materials must be crispy dry. Do not use plastic bowls or utensils, as they tend to absorb the fragrance. Gently mix all the dry ingredients together. Next, scatter drops of essential oil over the combined mixture using an eyedropper. Seal the mixture in an airtight container, stirring every two days. Allow curing for four to six weeks before displaying.

IF YOU ARE A TRUE POTPOURRI ENTHUSIAST
you might want to plant your own potpourri garden. Spring is the best time. Plants can be grown in a
rectangular bed, in borders in front of shrubs, in a
window box, or in a patio container, as well as on a
sunny windowsill indoors. Most plants enjoy the full
sun and need to be sheltered from the wind.

Harvest herbs and flowers late on a sunny morning after the evening moisture has evaporated. Air-
drying is the easiest way to make sure plant materials dry completely. Bundle like materials together.
Hang the bundles upside down in a dark, dry place
with good air circulation. Most will dry within a week
or two.

Here is a perfect recipe for creating a simple rose
potpourri mixture:

> *1 pint of dried roses*
> *1 ounce mixed herbs*
> *1/2 ounce orrisroot powder*
> *1 crumbled cinnamon stick*
> *1/2 teaspoon cloves*
> *1 star anise*
> *orange peel*
> *2 drops rose essential oil*
> *1 drop lavender essential oil*

**And let us not be weary in doing well: for in
due season we shall reap, if we faint not.**

—GALATIANS 6:9

THE DO-IT-YOURSELF CORSAGE
Joe Lamancusa

...

I WANTED A SMALL CORSAGE THAT MY WIFE,
Kathy, could wear to an evening reception. She loves flowers,
and she would be meeting some influential people in the pub-
lishing industry for the first time that night. I wanted to surprise her with a symbol of my love and support, something
tasteful that would make her appearance memorable to people she met.

We were staying in a very nice hotel in Los Angeles, so I
didn't think finding a corsage would be a problem. That was
my first mistake.

I assumed the hotel florist could create something fairly
quickly, so I waited until afternoon to head to the florist. The
minute I walked through the door, I sensed trouble. The florist
was visibly befuddled. When I asked if he could create a simple corsage with a few flowers for that evening, he responded
with a rampage of expletives about his assistant who hadn't
shown up and the huge event that night that he wasn't yet prepared for. A "simple" corsage for that evening? Was I kid-
ding?

Determined that Kathy would have flowers that night, I decided to take matters into my own hands! My eyes searched around the shop and landed on a few buckets of flowers on the floor, some stems of baby's breath on the counter, and a container of filled water tubes in the sink. I asked the florist if he would mind if I put a few flowers together myself. "Go ahead," he sniffed. Then he ignored me as he went about his work.

I selected some fragrant freesia, a few fern leaves, and some sprigs of baby's breath. After inserting each stem into a filled water tube, I grabbed a yard of peach satin corsage ribbon from the back shelf, tied a bow, and attached it to the flowers. I was so consumed with my work that I never noticed that the florist had been watching me.

"Are you a florist?" he asked. "If you are, I could really use some help here. Do you want a job for the night?"

I assured him that I was not a florist; I'd simply been surrounded by flowers and floral supplies for the better part of my life. Thanking him, I declined his offer of a job and then asked how much I owed him.

"I couldn't possibly charge you anything," he said sheepishly. "You did all the work." I thanked him again and wished him luck.

As I walked through the hall to the elevator and up to our room, I tried to think of something romantic to say to Kathy about her flowers. But nothing sounded better than the truth: The corsage had been created by my hands, with my love, against some interesting and comical odds. When she saw the corsage and listened to my story, she chuckled and said that it couldn't have been more beautiful.

When she went to pin it on for the evening, we realized that I had forgotten to get corsage pins. Kathy hunted and hunted until she found some safety pins in her makeup bag. We used them to attach the corsage from the inside of the dress!

The evening was wonderful. Kathy received many compliments on her corsage. And every time she did, she'd say "Thank you," look my way, and just smile.

FLOWER TYPES ARE BROKEN DOWN INTO FOUR categories, which constitute the entire range of flowers used in design: line flowers, mass flowers, filler flowers, and form flowers.

Line flowers are long, thin, tapering materials that are most often used at the extremities or outer portions of the design. Their purpose is to carry your eye through the design and also to establish the shape of the overall arrangement. Often these flowers will bring your eye to the center, or heart, of the design. Some examples of line flowers are: snapdragons, eucalyptus, and curly willow.

Mass flowers are usually the primary flowers used in a design. They are round, many-petaled flowers that are useful for filling space as well as for being the main feature of an arrangement. Sometimes they help to add bulk, variety, and texture. Some examples of mass flowers are: rose, carnation, and poppy.

Filler flowers are smaller flowers with many heads on one stem. The varieties are endless. Their purpose is to add a variation of color or texture, or to fill space in the design. Fillers need not be flowers. Materials such as leaves, ribbon loops, and bows are sometimes also considered fillers. Baby's breath is one example of a filler flower. There are many types of dried flowers available for use as fillers. Many of these are actually preserved instead of dried, making them more supple and easier to use.

Form flowers are unusual flowers, often with an elegant shape. They are used sparingly, and in ways that allow their beauty to be appreciated. Orchids are a good example of a form flower that is popular today.

All flowers appear to me as if coming from afar,
like news for which one hopes against hope.

—ANDRÉ DHÔTEL

FINISH LINE
Steve Moroski

. . .

ALTHOUGH MY WIFE, DEBRA, AND I LIVED IN
Atlanta all of our lives, it took a trip to Alaska for us to meet.
Under the midnight sun on June 21, 1997, at the finish line of
a marathon in Anchorage, we first laid eyes on each other. She
finished twenty seconds after I did. It was her birthday.

We continued with our passion for running marathons
while we were dating. When I decided to take the deep and
permanent plunge into spending the rest of my life with her, I
wanted to ask for her hand in marriage in a way she wouldn't
forget.

One year later, on June 21, 1998, we ran the San Diego
marathon together. I finished about five minutes ahead of her,
sweaty and exhausted; I sat down to wait. When Debra
crossed the line, she wasn't sweaty or exhausted, as I had
expected, but perky and smiling, ready to walk the half mile
to where our group of friends had agreed to meet after the
race. When we reached our friends, Deb immediately sat

down to chat with them. I asked one of my friends to take a walk with me because I wanted to show him something. I took him to where I had hidden twelve dozen roses for Debra. But rather than give all of them to her at the same time, I asked my friend to take a dozen roses over to Debra and tell her, "Good race." As he did that, I rounded up thirty people, some I knew and some I didn't, and asked each to take a handful of flowers and to do the same thing. Suddenly, people she didn't even know were coming at her from all sides, offering roses. She was speechless, shocked, and literally surrounded by flowers. She had no idea why this was happening, and the look on her face reminded me of how a little kid who has just been caught doing something wrong looks. I couldn't help smiling as I positioned myself behind all of the other rose givers. As my turn came closer and closer, I could feel the excitement growing. That's when I happened to look down at the heart monitor I always wear when I race. My heart rate had rocketed to 163, higher than it had been throughout the entire race!

Slowly, I walked up to my flower-covered girlfriend and handed her the last of the twelve dozen roses. I smiled, looked into her eyes, and said, "I want to run with you forever." I got down on one knee and asked, "Will you marry me?"

She didn't say anything right away. And as she leaned over to kiss me, I asked, "Is that a yes?" Debra smiled and said, "Of course, it's a yes!"

*And thou shalt be like a watered garden, and
like a spring of water, whose waters fail not.*

—ISAIAH 58:11

WEDNESDAY'S FLOWERS
Karen R. Peters

. . .

IT HAD BEEN A ROUGH SPRING. THE WORKERS
in my father's factory had gone on strike, and guards were stationed around the facilities to protect the people who chose to
come to work. With things at home so volatile, my father
thought it best that I stay on campus for the summer. At first,
the thought of staying at school was exciting. I was on track
to finish college a year early, and staying for the summer
could only help me meet my goal.

As summer school started, however, I began having trouble with my stomach and discovered that I had colitis. I was
put on a strict diet that consisted of Jell-O, rice, broth, and
plain chicken breasts. This was far worse than cafeteria food.
I became weak and tired from the endless barium drinks,
upper GI tests, and the unappetizing, bland food. I was in very
low spirits.

Then one Wednesday a bouquet of flowers was delivered
to the dorm for me. There was no note or card attached, no
florist's tag, no way of knowing who had sent the flowers.

There was only a small slip of paper on which my name was neatly typed. Assuming they had been sent by my father, I called to thank him, only to find out that he was not responsible. I then became a little Nancy Drew, scooping clues from friends and taking a fresh look at all the guys in my classes, trying to piece together the mystery and figure out who had sent the flowers. It rejuvenated me. I found myself analyzing every word spoken to me by possible suspects and discussing the conversations with my roommate, hoping that maybe she could help me discover who my secret admirer was.

Nearly a week had passed. The flowers had wilted, and still the giver did not present himself. Lost in my thoughts as I walked past the dorm office the next Wednesday, I heard someone holler, "You have another bouquet of flowers! Who's the new beau?" My face lit up. I grinned and replied, "I don't know!" With the second bouquet, the news soon spread to the other girls on our wing. Was it the quiet guy in my real estate class? The mysterious Iranian in my pottery class? But still there were no clues. Before long the second session of summer school would be over, and I thought for sure that my admirer would want to make himself known. But much to my surprise and dismay, the session ended without a hint.

But the flowers kept coming!

Every Wednesday for six weeks I received a bouquet of flowers. My clever questioning and careful determination had been to no avail, and I was running out of suspects. My roommate and I were no longer coy or careful detectives; we started asking guys directly if they had sent the flowers or knew

who had. But we were unsuccessful. We were glad that we
were business majors and not sleuths. At one point, I even
wondered if my roommate had sent the flowers to cheer me
up and then couldn't stop once the investigation involved
more and more people. But she assured me she hadn't been
that thoughtful.

But the flowers had lifted my spirits, despite my not
knowing who they were from. I no longer saw myself as a
tired and weak colitis patient trying to choke down a tasteless
diet, but as someone who was admired from afar. Every week
I eagerly anticipated the arrival of the flowers. They had
become an escape from an otherwise dull summer session,
filled with more work than play. The flowers brought healing
for my aching body, restoration to my soul, and sheer delight.
I was like a little girl collecting buttercups for my mother
instead of a much-too-serious twenty-year-old business student.

I never did discover who sent me the flowers. My roommate is still one of my dearest friends and has never confessed
to sending them. In fact, no one ever did confess. All I know
is that for six glorious Wednesdays I received a gift of much-
needed hope, a six-week bouquet of beauty, and an everlasting memory of that summer.

ATTRACTING HUMMINGBIRDS TO A GARDEN IS easy if you select the kinds of perennials they enjoy: columbine, coral bells, cardinal flower, lupine, and bee balm.

Perennials that dry well include yarrow, sneezewort, ornamental onion, pearly everlasting, astilbe, white mugwort, delphinium, globe thistle, sea holly, baby's breath, lavender, gayfeather, sea lavender, and lamb's ears.

Nor did I wonder at the lily's white,
Nor praise the deep vermilion in the rose;
They were but sweet, but figures of delight,
Drawn after you, —you pattern of all those.

—WILLIAM SHAKESPEARE

SURPRISE, SURPRISE!
Shirley M. Albertson

· · ·

MY HUSBAND OF THIRTY YEARS LEFT ME FOR another woman. I was devastated. Never angry, just hurt. I had trusted him. Over the years I became bitter and developed a "never again" attitude, deciding that I would never trust another man enough to become emotionally involved. I'd had enough pain.

After several years of being single, I met a man who asked me out to dinner. I was confused. The memories of being deceived flashed and crashed in my mind. *No,* I thought. *I do not want to get involved.* I put up my shield. But slowly the shield came down as I began to think about his invitation. *Yes,* I finally decided, figuring it was only dinner. I tossed my shield aside and accepted. We had a lovely evening, and I couldn't help thinking what a kind and considerate man I'd met.

After splitting up with my husband years earlier, it had dawned on me that I would never again know the joy of receiving flowers out of sheer love. Or so I thought. On my birthday, several months after my dinner date, a deliveryman from the local florist rang my doorbell and, to my surprise, presented me with two dozen red roses. A beautiful gift from my dinner friend.

I have since learned what a caring and thoughtful man I married. Yes, married. Fifteen years. I still receive flowers "just because," for no other reason than to express his love. He always sends roses or carnations, which I love, and he never forgets to write out a special, loving note.

And sometimes he gets creative about his flower buying and sending; rather than simply having the flowers delivered, he spontaneously thinks of ways to surprise me right under my nose! For instance, many times when we're shopping he'll make up an excuse to go off in another direction to do some shopping of his own. When we arrive home later on, he grins through the packages and hands me a bouquet of flowers he has been hiding in the car. The flowers are always surprisingly fresh because he never forgets to tell the florist to wrap them so they can sustain the car ride and all kinds of weather. Another time he took the car to the repair shop and decided to walk the two miles home. On the way, he stopped at the florist's and purchased three dozen red roses. I was amazed when he arrived home with such beautiful flowers, still in perfect shape after his long walk. I loved them—and the thought behind them.

I am so glad that I was brave enough to accept that dinner invitation all those years ago and that I was able start a new chapter in my life. Every Friday night my husband and I have a scheduled "date," and he wines and dines me just as if we were on our first date! We are in our sixties and seventies now, and I remain just as thrilled by his little boy grin today when he surprises me with bouquets of roses and carnations as I would have been at eighteen. Together, he and I, just like the flowers we both enjoy so much, bloom through the love we have in our hearts. Love and flowers bloom with nurturing.

FLOWER BULBS ARE AS INTERESTING TO DIS-play as their flowers are beautiful. Bulbs look better in a design if the dirt is washed off them. They can be cleaned in a bucket of water or rinsed under a water faucet. A garden hose can also do the trick if the weather is mild enough. Whatever method you choose, be careful of the roots; they are brittle and break easily.

Use a simple clear glass container to display the bulb with its twisted roots and peeling sheaf of paper skin. Place a handful of beach pebbles or washed gravel loosely in the bottom of the glass container. Add the bulb and add more pebbles or gravel gently around the roots. The most important thing is to give the root system a constant water source so the bulb will continue to thrive.

To the man who says kids bore him
flowers too are as nothing.

—BASHO

BIRTHDAY MIX-UP
Bernice Peitzer

• • •

MY HUSBAND, HERB, VOLUNTEERED TO CHAP-
eron our son's Boy Scout troop on a camping weekend during
the first week in June. That Sunday was my birthday, so Herb
asked if I minded spending it without them. I told him that I
didn't mind at all. I fondly remembered the camping trips I'd
taken with my Girl Scout troop and could not deny them that
wonderful, wholesome experience.

When I got up that Sunday morning, I could see a box
through the glass panel of our front door. Curiously, I opened
the door and was delighted to see a white florist's box tied
with a ribbon. My heart was beating with the excitement of
my husband's thoughtfulness. I hurried to open the box and
found inside a lovely nosegay with a cluster of white ribbons
cascading down. I was touched by Herb's simple sentiment
and took the sweet arrangement inside.

But as the hours rolled by I started thinking about that
nosegay, and I slowly realized that Herb would never send one
of those to me. I am a floral designer, and everyone in my fam-

ily knows that if a gift must be given, I'd prefer something other than flowers. And if he did decide to send flowers, it wouldn't be a nosegay; those are usually meant for little girls, not for a grown woman's birthday. Then it suddenly hit me: There must have been some mistake. Many times before, mail and other deliveries had come to my house by mistake. It was easy to confuse the name of my street with another that has a similar name. I immediately called the florist.

Yes, there had been a mistake. The flowers had, indeed, been delivered to the wrong house. That lovely nosegay was for a little girl who was going to be the flower girl at a wedding. It wasn't for me. The florist explained that the family of the little girl had called to say the nosegay hadn't been received and that another had been promptly sent out in its place. I had to laugh at myself as I told the florist that I had thought the nosegay was an odd but considerate birthday present for me. When I finished explaining, the florist said, "I wish you a very happy birthday. Enjoy it."

I grinned to myself as I hung up the phone, realizing that the flowers had made my day—despite the fact that they were meant for someone else. As I looked at the exquisite nosegay, I thought about my husband and son and the love they were sharing that weekend, and about the flower girl who had received an identical nosegay and the love she would witness that day at the wedding. I felt wonderfully complete, as though my birthday had already been celebrated.

PROPER CARE WILL ENSURE THAT YOUR FRESH bouquet brings you joy and happiness for many days—and sometimes several weeks.

To arrange a fresh bouquet of flowers, first fill a clear glass vase with room temperature water. Strip the stems of each flower so that no leaves will be covered by water. Leaves under the waterline will slowly rot and add bacteria to the water that are poisonous to the flowers.

Cut each stem about twice the height of the container, leaving several stems even a few inches longer to add height to the center of the arrangement. Always recut the stems of flowers to allow proper uptake of water.

Insert stems of foliage such as fern and filler flowers such as baby's breath first, crisscrossing the stems in the container to create a grid that will help hold the other flowers in place.

Starting around the outside edge of the vase, insert flowers, working your way to the center, where you will place the longest stems. Your design can be created with all one flower, such as roses, or with a mixture of varieties, such as daisies, carnations, lilies, and snapdragons.

If it were only to the eye that flowers were
beautiful they would still charm; but some-
times their scent, like a felicitous term of
existence, like a sudden call, leads toward a
return to a more intimate life.

—SENANCOUR

LESS IS MORE
Kirby Holt

. . .

TRICIA WALKED INTO MY LIFE THROUGH THE
doors of my floral shop, more radiant than the brightest rose
in the cooler.

She quickly became a very steady customer. It seemed that
flowers were a very important part of her life. Tricia would
buy flowers for a memorial, a birthday, a friend, another
friend. As time wore on, I remember thinking that Tricia was
more perfect than the most perfect woman I had ever imag-
ined. Beautiful, smart, savvy—and sexy, too!

After a few months of being one of my best customers, she came in with an unexpected request. She asked me
out!

As fate would have it, the concert tickets she had con-
flicted with a design show I had already scheduled. Was I dis-
appointed!

Shortly after, she asked again . . . another unbreakable commitment. I felt sick. But she was so interesting to me that I decided to ask her out a few days later. First she said, "No. You've already had two chances." She only paused an instant before breaking into a huge smile and quickly saying, "Yes!"

The first date was the usual pretending nervous encounter, but there was definitely some magic happening between us. After our second date— Wow! I was in love. It felt as if we were made for each other. The following Monday, I sent a fabulous garden floral design to her office with a one-word message—"Speechless." On Tuesday, I sent an abstract floral design with the message "Sleepless." Wednesday's arrangement arrived with the word "Breathless."

Tricia called on Wednesday afternoon and said, "You're not speechless, sleepless, or breathless—you're shameless!" So, of course, Thursday's floral design arrived with the message "Shameless." On Friday, the only emotion left to express was really an attitude—"Reckless."

That night she found the quarter-page ad I had placed in the local newspaper that said, "Yes, I am speechless, sleepless, breathless, totally shameless, and utterly reckless. You've made me the happiest man in the world."

One week later, during a walk down a country road, I pulled her into an alcove of trees covered with sweet honeysuckle from the sky to the forest floor. Dropping to both knees, I ceremoniously asked, "Tricia, will you marry me?" She smiled and said, "Kirby, you know I will, and I will make you the happiest man in the world."

We've been married for almost a year, and she has been true to her word—I am the happiest man in the world.

I'm so glad Tricia kept coming in to buy flowers—again, and again, and again. And I thank God for flowers; they help us to express our deepest feelings with their fabulous fleeting beauty.

Contributors

...

Shirley M. Albertson is an international artist and published poet who has received many honors for her poetry. She does speaking presentations and poetry readings of her own works to clubs, schools, universities, and symposiums. Shirley and her husband are the parents of three children and grandparents to six. She can be contacted at 419-994-4543.

Her favorite flower is the carnation.

Kathy Baker is president of A Few Choice Words, an Ohio company that specializes in inspirational, humorous, and spiritual writing and presentations. She is also a columnist for several publications. Kathy is married and has four children. Contact her at 330-678-3682, at <kabaker@bright.net>, or at <www.afewchoice words.net>.

Her favorite flower is the lilac.

Russ Barley, AAF, AIFD, is a floral designer and owner of Emerald Coast Flowers and Gifts in Santa Rosa Beach, Florida. He is the founder of the Emerald Coast Floral Association, is on the board of directors of the Florida State Floral Association, and is on the Who's Who National Register of Executives and Businesses. He was named 2000 Businessman of the Year of Walton County, Florida.

His favorite flower is the oncidium orchid.

Rochelle Beach has been married for thirty-three years to her sweetheart, John. She has four daughters and three grandchildren. She has worked with the youth of her church and teaches the Laurel class on Sundays. Rochelle has been a professional crafter for fourteen years, and owns and manages Cinna-Minnies Solid Cinnamon Collectibles. Cinna-Minnies are handmade dolls, ornaments, and home decor items made from a cinnamon clay that she developed. Mail inquiries to: Cinna-Minnies, 615 N. Saginaw St., Owosso, MI 48867, or visit <http://www.geocities.com/jocarte/Cinna-Minnies.html> for updates.

Her favorite flower is the rose.

Liz Bernstein is a wife and the mother of three daughters. Although she loves to be surrounded by flowers both inside and outside her home, the gardens that she has created in her mind far surpass those she has created in her yard!

Her favorite flower is French lavender.

Jill Boudreau, AIFD, is a freelance floral designer residing in southern Orange County, California. Her floral designs have been featured in *Flowers&* magazine and *Elan* magazine. She enjoys wedding work and presents a design program titled "Fragrance and Flowers." She can be contacted at 949-366-3791.

Her favorite flower is her grandmother's sweet peas.

Kathleen Bretherick, NDSF, is a past president of the Society of Floristry in England. She has held the Society Diploma since 1957. A chief examiner and city and guilds assessor, she organizes flower demonstrations and shows, and has judged floristry throughout the country. Fifty years ago she established the firm of Brethericks, and now she and her daughter and business partner, Sandra, run two shops. She is the author of numerous books on floristry. She can be reached at 180 Harrogate Road, Leeds LS7 4NZ, West Yorkshire, England.

*Her favorite flowers are the rubrum lily
and the white gardenia.*

Arnold "Nick" Carter, CSP, CPAE, of Deerfield, Illinois, is VP Emeritus of Communications Research for the Nightingale-Conant Corporation. He has an M.A. in human communications and has received highest honors from the National Speakers Association, the CSP, and CPAE. His aim is to bring people to success and happiness. Contact him at 800-572-2770, ext. 2236, or 847-647-7145 (fax).

His favorite flower is the red rose.

Elisabeth Charles enjoys her various roles as wife, mother, and VP of marketing at joann.com, an exciting and unique online arts and crafts and home decor web site.

Her favorite flower is the rubrum lily.

Lynn Downing lives in northeastern Ohio with her husband, Blaine. She enjoys hiking, making craft projects, and frequenting flea markets and estate sales. She doesn't know what she wants to be when she grows up, but she is sure it will involve working with kids.

Her favorite flower is the snapdragon.

Poul Einsbøj and his wife, Karen, have worked with flowers and floristry for more than thirty years, Karen as a florist, Poul with Smithers-Oasis, a major manufacturer and supplier of floral foam and accessories for the floral industry. They are Danish and have lived and worked with their family in Germany, and are now settled in Great Britain.

His favorite flower is the tulip.

Tim Farrell, AAF, is a retail florist in Drexel Hill, Pennsylvania, serving the southwestern suburbs of Philadelphia. He is married with three children. Tim is active in the floral industry. He is a past president of the Penn Jersey Unit of Teleflora, the current Regional Unit Director of Teleflora for the northeastern United States, a member of the educational committee of the Pennsylvania Floral Industry Association, and a 2000 inductee to the American Institute of Floral Designers.

His favorite flower is the tulip, of course!

Carolina Fernandez, M.B.A., worked at IBM and as a stockbroker with Merrill Lynch before she started her family. She now runs a home-based business marketing a line of custom-designed, hand-painted children's playwear that bears her name. She has written her first book on creative motherhood and is active in a wide variety of writing and public speaking platforms that allow her the opportunity to encourage mothers and inspire their creativity. She lives with her husband, Ernie, and children Nicolas, Benjamin, Cristina, and Victor in Ridgefield, Connecticut. Contact her at 203-894-8977; at <www.carolinafernandez.com>; or at <emomrx @yahoo.com>.

Her favorite flower is the pink rose.

Elaine Gartner, wife and mother of three, is a director of technology in an upstate New York school district. Because of allergies, she views flowers only from afar but is an avid vegetable and fruit tree gardener. She can be reached at <tech_usa@excite.com>.

Her favorite flower is the tiger lily—
particularly wild ones.

Nori Gartner-Baca and her husband, John, live in Orange County, New York, where they are looking forward to building their first home. Nori works in nonprofit public relations, designing and writing publications for schools. In her free time, she enjoys writing fiction and volunteering at a children's library.

Her favorite flower is the calla lily.

Barbara Glanz, CSP, is an internationally known author and professional speaker who works with organizations that want to improve morale and with people who want to rediscover the joy in their work and in their lives. She is the author of *CARE Packages for the Home, CARE Packages for the Workplace, The Creative Communicator,* and *Building Customer Loyalty.* Her topic areas include "Regenerating Spirit in the Workplace and in the Home" and "Building Customer Loyalty." Contact her at 708-246-8594; at <bglanz@barbaraglanz. com>; or at <www.barbaraglanz.com>.

Her favorite flower is the gardenia.

Charles Goodwin is a retired architect with three grown children and five grandchildren. He loves gardening; spending time with his wife, Rose; and playing with his grandchildren.

His favorite flower is the iris.

Alice E. Heim is a professional needlecraft designer specializing in tatted and crocheted lace; she has written two books, *DMC Bridal Tatting* and *Crochet for Wedding and Home.* She and her husband, Dal, have two daughters and four grandchildren.

Her favorite flowers are daffodils and roses.

Donna Herrin is a wife and the mother of two girls, aged eleven and thirteen, and lives in Twinsburg, Ohio. She is currently working in the kitchen of the Valley Christian Academy and is a part-time wedding coordinator. Donna finds gardening relaxing, and enjoys writing and public speaking, which she hopes to pursue more seriously in the future.

Her favorite flower is the daffodil.

Kirby Holt, AIFD, has had a lifelong passion for flowers, so after many years of being in retail management he chose to become a floral designer. He is the owner of Blossoms in Chipley, Florida. Kirby is the 2000 president of the Florida Panhandle Florists'

Association. Along with presenting design shows and educational forums across the Southeast, he teaches floral design at community and technical colleges in Florida and Alabama. Contact him at 850-638-7786.

His favorite flower is the stargazer lily.

Diane Gunn Hurd, M.B.A., and her husband, John, own and operate Avatar's World, a dried flower wholesale company. They also publish and sell a book about starting your own cut flower business called *Field Grown Cut Flowers.* They grow and sell fresh-cut flowers, including peonies and hydrangeas, bridal wreath, and cranberry bush. You can contact her at 608-884-4730 or e-mail <avatar@inwave. com>. Visit her web site, <www.avatarsworld.com>.

Her favorite flower is the gardenia.

Christina Keating is a physical therapist in Queens, New York. She is an avid baseball fan and enjoys spending time with her husband and friends.

Her favorite flower is the orchid.

Joe Lamancusa is the husband of the author of this book. Along with being the business manager of Kathy's speaking career, he is the owner of Visual Design Concepts, an advertising, marketing, and consulting business with clients in the floral, craft, and creative industries. He is also the president of Creative Directions, Inc., a company through which readers can order additional books and videos by Kathy Lamancusa. Contact him at 330-494-7224 or <joe@lamancusa.com>. Also visit <www.lamancusa.com>.

His favorite flower is the iris.

Larry Laney is a retired U.S. Marine Corps gunnery sergeant living with his wife, Daryl, and son, Chris, in Massillon, Ohio. He is an avid golfer and amateur gardener.

His favorite flower is the rose.

Hope Mihalap, CPAE, is a Greek from Virginia and a professional humorist married to a Russian. She has received the Mark Twain Award for Humor and the Speaker Hall of Fame Award from the National Speakers Association—the Oscar of her profession. Hope can be reached at 757-640-0333 or <hopehumor@whro.net>.
Her favorite flower is the lily of the valley.

Steve Moroski of Atlanta, Georgia, is the author of *Stay Hungry.* As a speaker, he helps organizations embrace change and drive sales. Contact him at 770-329-2990 or <steve@moroski.com>.
His favorite flower is the rose.

Lynne Moss, AIFD, PFCI, AAF, is a retail floral designer from Pratt, Kansas. Being from America's heartland keeps Lynne close to nature. She enjoys sharing her creativity, which she feels comes from the heart and soul of her flowers, with customers. She can be contacted at 316-672-7231 or at <flwrshop@prattflowers.com>.
Her favorite flower is the tulip.

Alice-Lynne Olson owns the Late Bloomer Floral Design Studio in Edina, Minnesota. She is a freelance designer specializing in special events and wedding designs for an average of 150 to 200 weddings annually. She became the Late Bloomer when she enrolled in floral design school after being laid off from a corporate banking career and discovered her true passion for weddings and floral design.
Her favorite flower is the peony.

Cynthia Panton is a freelance researcher and writer. She works as a counselor and teacher at Cleveland State University. History, romance, and the past are her particular favorites. Contact her at <c.panton@csuohio.edu>.
Her favorite flower is the camellia.

Alan Parkhurst, AIFD, PFCI, has twenty-five years in the floral industry and is a noted speaker and designer. He is the National Floral Design Manager for Jo-Ann Stores. Contact him at 330-722-2907.

His favorite flower is the iris.

Bernice Peitzer is a professional designer of pressed flowers, a lecturer, and the author of *Forever Flowers—From Seed to Designing, Plus 45 Keepsake Projects.* She is president of Peitzer Floral Arts, West Orange, New Jersey. One of her specialties is designing a pressed flower arrangement on invitations. Contact her at <BernPei@juno.com>.

Her favorite flower is the rose-colored
double-petal peony.

Karen R. Peters is a wife and the mother of three sons. She enjoys gardening, entertaining, and teaching Bible studies. Karen often uses gardening concepts to illustrate biblical truths. She can be contacted at <KRPeters10@hotmail.com>.

Her favorite flower is the gerbera daisy.

Kathy Peterson is host of her own national TV show, *Town & Country Crafts with Kathy Peterson;* author; designer; columnist; contributing editor; and more. Contact her through her web site at <www.kathypeterson.com>. She can be contacted at <kp@kathy peterson.com> or call 561-744-2086.

Her favorite flower is the peony.

Andrew Pike is a student in Minnesota pursuing a career in law enforcement and motivational speaking. His life motto is "Carpe Diem—Seize the Day . . . and live it to the fullest." Andrew can be contacted at <Sttetroopr@aol.com>.

His favorite flower is the snowdrop.

Terrilynn Quillen is a nurse, writer, and craft designer who recently returned to college to complete the baccalaureate in nursing that was interrupted when she met and married "the man with the orange rose." Twenty years and two kids later, they're still living "happily ever after." Terri is still involved in intercessory prayer ministry. She prays that all the single people reading this book will, too, find God's gift of "true love" in their lives. Readers are welcome to share their prayer requests by writing to Terri at PMB N-161, 3100 Meridian Park Drive, Greenwood, IN 46142.

Her favorite flower is the sweetheart rose.

Angela Ronemark is a wife and the mother of two young sons who keep her very busy. She enjoys being a stay-at-home mom and planting gardens of flowers.

Her favorite flower is the bleeding heart.

Rosemarie Rossetti, Ph.D., is a professional speaker, trainer, consultant, and writer. As an inspirational speaker, she demonstrates how people can move from fear to hope by turning adversity into opportunities. As a trainer, she works with organizations that want their people to communicate clearly and with people who want to feel at ease in front of a group. Contact her in Columbus, Ohio, at 614-471-6100 or online at <Rosemarie@RosemarieSpeaks.com>. Or visit her web site, <www.RosemarieSpeaks.com>.

Her favorite flower is the phalaenopsis orchid.

Cheryl Runstrom is the busy mother of five and a proud navy officer's wife. She and her family are currently stationed in Virginia.

Her favorite flower is the yellow rose.

Nada Rutka, ASID, CMG, is principal of Nada Associates, a color design consultancy in Canonsburg, Pennsylvania. As a color designer, she takes the guesswork out of color selection for manu-

factured products. For more information on color design, visit
<www.colordesigner.com>.

Her favorite flower is the Peace rose.

JoAnn C. Schleis is a freelance designer and teacher in the arts
and crafts industry. She enjoys her family, travel, and genealogy. She
may be contacted at <schleis@willinet.net>.

Her favorite flower is the pink rose.

Elaine Schmidt is a design, product development, and marketing
consultant in the creative crafts industry. Her original designs have
been featured in a wide variety of magazines and books, as well as
on television. She is a member of the Hobby Industries of America
and the Society of Craft Designers. Elaine can be contacted at
<ESDesigns@aol.com>.

Her favorite flower is the gerbera daisy.

Lillian Sibila is a widow with four grown sons. She is a charter
member and past president of her garden club and has been attending for forty-five years. She enjoys her eight grandchildren, watercolor painting, gardening, and flower arranging.

Her favorite flower is a rose that she started
under a quart jar in 1946 from a cutting taken
from her parents' home. It is a beautiful
old-fashioned light pink.

Shirley Sluis, AIFD, is a widow with four grown children. She
has been in the floral industry for thirty-six years. Shirley operated a
flower shop with her sister in Bethel, Connecticut, for twenty-two
years and now works part-time for Timeless Elegance in Orange
Park, Florida. She also does freelance work and loves to give demonstrations and teach floral design.

Her favorite flowers are pink or peach roses.

Craig Sole, AIFD, is a special events florist in Overland Park, Kansas. His shop is in a 1920s bungalow surrounded by the flowers he loves to design with in his daily work.

His favorite flower is Queen Anne's lace.

Janice Stucky decorates her house every year with at least a dozen different Christmas trees of all shapes and sizes. She hides gifts under each one for her husband. She works as a bank teller and enjoys her husband and two cocker spaniels.

Her favorite flower is the camellia.

Susan E. Warkentin, P. Eng., is a professional mechanical engineer with subsequent diplomas in fashion design and education. For the past twelve years her day job has been revealing the finer points of mathematics to high school students in Ontario, Canada. Outside the classroom, she can be found herding her two children to sports, writing, painting watercolors, stenciling, sewing, or deeply immersed in a good book. Her husband is gradually being won over to the fabulous world of flowers. She may be contacted at <susawark @log.on.ca>.

Her favorite flowers are
alstroemeria for arrangements and
daylilies in the garden.

Paula Westbrook is a former high school business, English, and special education teacher. She is currently a domestic goddess (wife and mom) with three children. She resides in Alvarado, Texas. Contact her at 817-790-2324 or <DomesticGoddess23@hotmail. com>.

Her favorite flower is the yellow rose.

Karen Wingard is a part-time office secretary at Jackson Friends Church in Massillon, Ohio, where she and her husband are members. Karen enjoys spending the rest of her time at her twenty-acre country home with her dogs, cats, cows, husband, and son.
Her favorite flower is the daisy.

Kathy G. Wise, RD, LD, is a registered dietitian with extensive experience in creating nutrition and wellness programs for hospitals, corporations, and individuals. Kathy serves as a nutrition consultant for restaurants, chefs, grocery stores, physicians, companies, and individuals. She is a noted public speaker on nutrition and is frequently interviewed for television, radio, and newspapers. Kathy separates the fads from the facts and gives professional support to people in the process of achieving a healthier lifestyle. Contact her at 330-497-1882. Also visit <www.anutritionchoice.com>.
Her favorite flowers are yellow Peace roses and sweetheart roses.

Julie Woodell enjoys life with her husband and children. She works part-time as a receptionist and brings flowers to work every week.
Her favorite flower is the hibiscus.

Linda Wyszynski is a freelance needlework designer, teacher, and needlepoint canvas painter living in Golden Valley, Minnesota. Her designs are published in leading needlework and craft magazines. Contact her at 612-545-1009.
Her favorite flower is the rose.

Lillian Zarzar, from Columbus, Ohio, is the founder of MIND-SHIFT. Her workshops and consultations assist individuals and organizations to shift perceptions, enhance inspirations, and increase awareness. She is the author of *Appleosophy: Slices of*

Apple-Inspired Wisdom and co-author of *Breakthrough Secrets to Live Your Dreams.* Contact her at 614-486-5523 or <lilzarzar @aol.com>. She is available for personal consultations and group presentations.

Her favorite flower is the red rose.

Contributors' Earned Designations

A A F

American Academy of Floriculture is an honor that is achieved by individuals meeting the academy's high standards of service to the industry and community.

A I F D

The American Institute of Floral Designers is the floral industry's leading nonprofit organization committed to establishing and maintaining higher standards in professional floral design. With nearly 1,000 members worldwide, AIFD and its members are in the forefront of the industry in presenting educational and design programs. Membership in AIFD is selective. To be accepted, a candidate must fulfill rigid qualifications and demonstrate advanced professional ability. Applicants must successfully complete a two-part process in which they prove their design abilities, first through a portfolio of photographs, and then through an actual on-site design.

A S I D

The American Society of Interior Designers (ASID), headquartered in Washington, D.C., is the oldest and largest professional organization representing both commercial and residential interior designers. With more than 30,500 members, ASID establishes a common identity for professionals and businesses in the field of design. ASID provides its members with ongoing support, education, and resources.

The association has forty-nine chapters throughout the United States and more than 450 international members. ASID was founded in 1975 with the consolidation of the American Institute of Designers (AID) and the National Society of Interior Designers (NSID). ASID promotes professionalism in interior design services and products for the work, home, learning, and commercial environments. The society's online service at <www.asid.org> features specialized information, news bulletins, membership information, reports, publications, product options/availability, and more.

C M G

Color Marketing Group (CMG), founded in 1962 and based in Alexandria, Virginia, is an international not-for-profit association of 1,600 color designers. Color designers are professionals who enhance the function, salability, and/or quality of a product through their knowledge and appropriate application of color. CMG members forecast color directions one to three years in advance for all industries, manufactured products, and services. These consumer/residential and contract/commercial products include: interior/exterior home; transportation; architectural/building; communications/graphics; fashion; action/recreation; and environments for office, health care, retail, and hospitality/entertainment.

CPAE SPEAKER HALL OF FAME

Established in 1977 by the National Speakers Association, the *Council of Peers Award of Excellence (CPAE Speaker Hall of Fame)* is a lifetime award for speaking excellence and professionalism given to speakers who have been evaluated by their peers and been judged to have mastered seven categories: material, style, experience, delivery, image, professionalism, and communication.

C S P

The Certified Speaking Professional designation, established in 1980 by the National Speakers Association, is the speaking industry's international measure of professional platform skill. In addition to their proven track record of continuing speaking experience and expertise, CSPs are committed to ongoing education, outstanding service, and ethical behavior. The CSP designation is conferred only on those accomplished speakers who have earned it by meeting strict criteria, including: serving at least 100 different clients within a five-year period; presenting at least 250 professional speaking engagements within the same five-year period; and submitting testimonial letters from clients served.

M. B. A.

Master's Degree in Business Administration

N D S F

National Diploma of the Society of Floristry in England

NSA: The Voice of the Speaking Profession

The National Speakers Association (NSA) is an international association of more than 3,800 members dedicated to advancing the art and value of experts who speak professionally. For more than twenty-five years NSA has provided resources and education designed to enhance the business acumen and platform performance of professional speakers. Please visit NSA's web site at <www.nsaspeaker.org>.

P. Eng.

Professional Engineer

PFCI

Professional Floriculture Commmentators International serves as an industry resource for floral commentators and educators. The PFCI designation signifies a dedication to excellence in floral commentary, leadership, knowledge, and commitment to personal and industry goals.

SCD

The Society of Craft Designers promotes the professional excellence of its members through educational opportunities and forums for career growth within the craft design industry. It was founded in 1975, as a professional organization for those who believe that quality craft design is the basis of a strong and viable craft industry. It is the only membership organization exclusively serving those who design for the consumer craft industry. They can be contacted at: P.O. Box 3388, Zanesville, OH 43702-3388: Phone: 740-452-4541. Fax: 740-452-2552

ABOUT THE AUTHOR

Kathy Lamancusa likes making a difference through ideas and inspiration. She shares new perspectives and adds creative sparks of energy in her work as a professional speaker, author, floral designer, television host, and media personality. Kathy is also proud to be a mother, wife, quilter, and gardener.

She speaks internationally to thousands each year about a wide variety of motivational and business topics. The focuses of her motivational presentations include: understanding current lifestyle, design, and color trends; establishing family traditions and values; balancing life through gardening principles; nurturing relationships and connections; celebrating the experiences of life; and overcoming challenges, as well as enhancing and fostering creativity. She often incorporates flowers into her presentations. Kathy also speaks to business audiences about current trends, sensory forces, visual merchandising, and promotion.

Kathy has written more than thirty-six instructional books and produced fifty flower arranging and wedding floral design instructional videos that are sold internationally. More than 1.5 million of Kathy's books have been sold.

Her television show, *Kathy Lamancusa's at Home with Flowers,* has aired on PBS stations around the United States. Kathy has also appeared as a guest on shows that air on Home & Garden Television, the Discovery Channel, the Learning Channel, TNN, CBN, CNN, and the four major networks.

She is a freelance writer and editor who works with international trade and consumer magazines, editing and providing designs and articles on lifestyle and color trends.

Kathy lives with her husband, Joe, in North Canton, Ohio. When not traveling, she enjoys being at home, studying the stars from the center of her hot tub, reading with a hot cup of tea, and walking through the garden. Her two sons, Joe and Jim, are young adults who are studying and traveling the world. Her favorite flowers include lilacs and daisies.

SHARE THE IMPACT OF FLOWERS

Was there a time in your life when flowers brought you joy, gave you a hug, or helped you send a message of hope, love, friendship, or celebration? I would love to hear your special story. I am planning future books that will feature stories to illustrate the profound effect flowers have on life, celebrations, love, romance, passion, and sorrow.

I am seeking heartwarming stories, reflections, and memories of up to three pages in length to include in these volumes. I am also very interested in including little-known information about the care and handling of flowers, tips for surrounding yourself with flowers, and garden advice.

I invite you to join me in these future projects by sending your stories and information for special consideration. If your story is selected for inclusion, you will be listed as a contributor and may include a biographical paragraph. Send your submissions to:

CREATIVE DIRECTIONS, INC.
FLORAL MEMORIES
8755 CLEVELAND AVENUE
NORTH CANTON, OH 44720

You can also make submissions by e-mail to: <editor@laman cusa.com>.

SHARE THE IMPACT OF QUILTS

Quilts speak to us with a language uniquely their own. They comfort us, help us preserve memories, and provide us a means of sharing with others in ways that touch the heart and soul. I would love to hear your special story. I am planning future books that will feature stories illustrating the profound effect quilts have on all aspects of our life.

I am seeking heartwarming stories, reflections, and memories of up to three pages in length to include in these volumes. I am also very interested in including little-known information about the care and handling of quilts, as well as tried-and-true quilting tips and techniques.

I invite you to join me in sharing the profound message of quilts by sending your stories and information for special consideration. If your story is selected for inclusion, you will be listed as a contributor and may include a biographical paragraph. Send your submissions to:

CREATIVE DIRECTIONS, INC.
QUILT MEMORIES
8755 CLEVELAND AVENUE
NORTH CANTON, OH 44720

You can also make submissions by e-mail to: <editor@laman
cusa.com>.

"FRIDAY'S FLOWERS" E-MAIL NEWSLETTER

If you want to be touched by more stories, memories, tips, and ideas related to flowers, subscribe to our free e-mail newsletter, "Friday's Flowers." Each Friday you will receive a snippet of floral information or a short story about flowers directly on your desktop to get you ready for your weekend! To enroll, send a "subscribe Friday's Flowers" message to <info@lamancusa.com>.

PRESENTATIONS

Kathy speaks to audiences around the world. She is familiar to many people because of her television and media appearances, her magazine columns, and her 1.5 million books in print. Her warm, energetic presentation style is inspirational as it motivates audiences to appreciate life more fully.

She shares the celebrations and challenges of life, and the focuses of her various presentations include: establishing family traditions and values, nurturing relationships and connections, appreciating celebrations and overcoming challenges, and nurturing and enhancing creativity.

Kathy's content-rich presentations are exhilarating, results-oriented, and highly inspirational as she stimulates creative approaches to life. With commonsense wisdom and contagious humor, she offers specific how-to's and action plans so that audiences can immediately implement her highly valuable information.

Kathy customizes each keynote, breakout, workshop, or spouse program, incorporating the information that will be most appropriate to the needs of the audience.

For more information on booking Kathy to speak to your group, visit her web site at <www.lamancusa.com> or call 330-494-7224.